5 Days *to a*
Clutter-Free
House

Other Books by Sandra Felton

Organizing for Life
Living Organized

Other Books by Sandra Felton and Marsha Sims

Organizing Your Day
Smart Office Organizing

5 Days *to a* Clutter-Free House

Quick, Easy Ways to
Clear Up Your Space

Sandra Felton
and Marsha Sims

a division of Baker Publishing Group
Grand Rapids, Michigan

Published by Revell
a division of Baker Publishing Group
P.O. Box 6287, Grand Rapids, MI 49516-6287
www.revellbooks.com

Printed in the United States of America

Library of Congress Cataloging-in-Publication Data
Felton, Sandra.
    5 days to a clutter-free house : quick, easy ways to clear up your space / Sandra Felton and Marsha Sims.
        pages cm
    Summary: "A professional organizer and a time-management expert team up to create a plan to de-clutter your home in five days" Provided by publisher.
    ISBN 978-0-8007-2107-7 (pbk. : alk. paper)
    1. Storage in the home. 2. House cleaning. 3. Time management. I. Sims, Marsha. II. Title. III. Title: Five days to a clutter-free house : quick, easy ways to clear up your space.
TX309.F45 2013
641.4'8—dc23   2012034360

Scripture quotations are from the King James Version of the Bible.

To protect the privacy of those who have shared their stories with the authors, some details and names have been changed.

The internet addresses, email addresses, and phone numbers in this book are accurate at the time of publication. They are provided as a resource. Baker Publishing Group does not endorse them or vouch for their content or permanence.

In keeping with biblical principles of creation stewardship, Baker Publishing Group advocates the responsible use of our natural resources. As a member of the Green Press Initiative, our company uses recycled paper when possible. The text paper of this book is composed in part of post-consumer waste.

13   14   15   16   17   18   19   7   6   5   4   3   2   1

From Sandra: To my family—my husband, Ivan, and the kids, now grown, Lucy, Peter, and Doug, who were all a part of the mix at the house as we moved from a cluttered to a clear way of life. And for the freedom from the grip of disorganization, I say with a heartfelt Miami-type thanks to the Lord, *"Gracias a Dios! Muchas gracias!"*

From Marsha: This book is dedicated to my three sons, George, Charles, and Darryl, who forced me to learn how to declutter my home quickly. They taught me how to use tough love and to create strategies that guided them toward the decision that they would rather clean up their own spaces than accept my creative consequences. And to my extended family of sons, Jabbar, Jimmy, Chris, Eugene, Garry, and Sadiki, who were always around. We all had fun and learned how to clean up and organize together.

Contents

Contents

Preface

As professional organizers, we believe that the disorganized people we have dealt with are among the greatest people in the world. Creative, relationship-focused, intelligent, and warmly sentimental, they are wonderful people to know.

We include ourselves in the group of people who are disorganized by nature. The only difference between us and those we seek to help is that through training and by the grace of God, we have recovered. Our own backgrounds as inborn disorganized folks are excellent credentials, because we have had to learn from scratch. We're able to break down the causes of and cures for clutter in a way organized people couldn't begin to fathom.

In our many years of experience, disorganized people have impressed us with their many good—very good—qualities. Often it is these very qualities that lead them into the cluttered condition of their houses. As we look around their homes, we note they are:

- Intelligent—Oh, so many books and papers!
- Curious—Magazines, newspapers, and time on the Internet
- Productive—Many half-done projects in the works
- Appreciative of beauty—Displays galore of favorite things
- Frugal—Items retained "just in case" they might be needed
- Helpful—Things kept in the event someone else needs them
- Creative—Hobbies and crafts inspire them
- Careful—Abundant receipts, sale offers
- Loving—Pets, sometimes lots and lots of pets

These very qualities are what make the disorganized such lovable and enjoyable people. Unfortunately, these qualities also lead disorganized people toward a way of life that stifles the expression of who they are.

If you can't easily find the things you want and need, frustration clouds the enjoyment of what you are trying to do. Even though you are warm and friendly, the messy house places a barrier between you and your friends and family. And then, of course, a messy and disorganized house is not inviting; it is not a place for you to relax and rejuvenate. Instead, it demands that you spend time and energy on trying to make some sort of improvement—to make your house a home.

You deserve better than that. You *can* have a home that refreshes and inspires you—you simply need to follow what we've dubbed the Mount Rushmore method. It's a five-day "toe-to-head" approach that will create a totally different and enjoyable life of order and beauty.

Building Your Organizing Vocabulary

When we talk organizing, we often use words that may be unfamiliar. When we use the term *Mount Rushmore*, we're talking about a unique organizing method created to get your house in order in five days. The "rush" part means the job gets done quickly. The "more" part means you don't try to do the job alone; you get help. We'll explain the process fully in the first section of the book.

Using a team approach is an important part of the power of this program. When we speak of a Clean Team, we mean bringing in outside forces to help move things from cluttered to clean. A "team" may be only one other person, but ideally it should consist of a few more, enough to get the assigned activities of the day done throughout the house.

> **GOD'S RECOMMENDATION OF TEAMWORK**
>
> Two are better than one; because they have a good reward for their labour.
>
> For if they fall, the one will lift up his fellow: but woe to him that is alone when he falleth; for he hath not another to help him up.
>
> Ecclesiastes 4:9–10 (KJV)

When we discuss maintenance, we mean keeping the house organized consistently after it has been de-cluttered. The second section of the book covers that topic.

What About Guys?

People sometimes ask, "Why are your books written primarily to women, since guys are just as messy, or messier?"

Most women know the answer. Whether we like it or not, women usually care more and carry more responsibility for the house than men. How do we know? Just look around. An Internet group designed for messy men closed for lack of interest. Classes on organizing have a dozen women for every man. Women's magazines have articles about organizing in every issue. Do you see this kind of article in men's magazines? We think not.

We include a guy now and then in our references because they often need the same kind of help—they're just not as plentiful when it comes to asking for organizational assistance. Messies Anonymous (www.messies.com) does offer a small ebook called *Messy Men Clean Up Their Act*. So men, you are welcomed into the ranks of those who want to move from cluttered to clear. Just don't be surprised that your fellow male comrades are few.

About This Book

Our purpose in writing this book is to help you move to a new way of life from the clutter that surrounds you. It is for those who are somewhat or significantly cluttered. Keep in mind that an obsessive clutterer may require more significant intervention. But if you have hope and are game, we'll help you usher in comfort you could never have imagined in your house and will never want to abandon.

This book has two sections:

- Section 1 details the five-day program.
- Section 2 explains how to keep your newly ordered house under control.

Thanks to all who contributed by letting us into their hearts and houses. The people are real. When we asked for their experiences with team cleaning, many of them wrote to us, telling how the approach you will read about impacted their lives. We include their writings just as they came to us. They reflect genuine sincerity. Some of our examples are from hands-on, in-the-trenches organizing experiences. Some are composites. Care has been taken to protect the identity of each.

Envious of Having a Team

Maryann set the stage for where we are going when she wrote:

> "I'm looking forward to the book. I often wonder how to handle all the paperwork and stuff I have amassed over the years. I hate to think of my passing and leaving my family this situation. I confess, I have been envious of those who could have a team come in and take over. I'm so looking forward to the book!"

So let's get started!

Introduction

What You Need to Know to Get Started

Have you ever wanted to be on one of those clean-up-your-mess-in-a-jiffy reality TV shows? *That would be so quick and easy,* you think. *I wish they could come to my house.*

Now you can have the same experience—only better. You'll be the producer, assembling the crew and orchestrating the whole show. No strangers in the house. No embarrassment with cameras. No inconvenient timetable. Just good results. A neat, organized house in a remarkably quick time.

That's what this book is about: overcoming trouble, the kind of trouble that clutter brings to your life in one way or another. Like when all or many of the surfaces of your house are cluttered with misplaced items. Like when you hesitate to invite people in. Like when you are sick and tired of the mess and just want to live a clear, clutter-free life. If you're at that point, you've come to the right place. Soon you will be able to breathe a large sigh of relief and inhale the joy of clutter-free rooms.

That's what Renee wanted. She had one of those "special rooms" that was full of debris, boxes, and overstuffed trash bags she'd been meaning to get to (for years). There were surfaces of her house that she couldn't use for their intended purpose because they were peppered with papers and miscellaneous items. She was tired of her family complaining. But mostly she was tired of living this way herself. The house didn't look good, and it didn't work right. She was simply ready to make a change. This book is for Renee. And if you can relate, this book is for you, too.

> **Stop and ask yourself this all-important question: "If everything were perfect and my house were set up exactly the way I want it, what would it look like?" Imagine it!**

First, we'll discuss the problems of clutter. Then, we'll move quickly on to how you can have clear surfaces and easy-to-find belongings in just a week. *Speed* is our watchword, because it offers the best guarantee of success. In the past you may have started but ground to a stop before the job was done. That won't happen with this plan.

It may sound like magic. But you really can, and will, have a new house in a very short time, and you will learn to keep it that way.

The Big Question That Makes This Program Work

The first important step in working the magic to create your new house is this all-important question: "If everything were perfect and your house were set up exactly the way you want it, what would it look like?"

Take time to ponder it deeply right now. You have to have a firm idea of where you want to go. In sports, many athletes visualize themselves winning. Speakers see a standing ovation in their minds. Young people who are in tune to their future career success often picture themselves in the position they hope to attain. You, in your quest for a clutter-free home, will benefit from doing the same.

Be sure to take a few seconds or more to visualize your table empty, your counter clear, and your floor debris-free before you enthusiastically begin to de-clutter any part of your house. Though it may not seem to be all that important, the step of visualization is vital to success.

Embracing the vision of your perfect house begins the change process in your thinking and your behavior—and helps you to continue maintaining order and beauty. Therefore, we hope you will make this foundational step a permanent part of your thinking long after the book is through.

Blythe kept hitting a wall in her efforts to keep her home clutter-free. It wasn't that she didn't try; she did. But it seemed that no matter how hard she tried, the clothes somehow ended up in piles on the bed, shoe pairs separated and spread across the floor, the bathroom counter perpetually crowded with makeup. As soon as she would get her kitchen countertop cleaned off and organized, it would slowly creep back into disarray. All of her hard efforts melted and she would have to do a marathon sprint cleanup again. It was a miserable yo-yo experience, and she began to think that she would never, ever be able to keep her house in order. But somewhere along the way, somebody suggested that imagining a goal was a very powerful force. At first she thought it was a silly and unnecessary step. But because it took only a few seconds, she surrendered her objections and gave it a try. What did she have to lose?

To her surprise, she found that once she had "seen" an area empty, she was able to recognize what items didn't belong there, and she removed them immediately. It made all the difference. The cluttered areas remained clear in a way they never had before.

Sit for a while and meditate on the details of how your perfect house would look. If you are in the habit of writing in a journal, or even in a blog or social media page, spell out what kind of house would make your heart jump with happiness when you open the front door after a hard day away. Start your writing, "I see my dream house. It has . . ."

- clear surfaces
- harmonious colors (your favorites)
- well-placed furniture
- uncluttered kitchen counters and a picked-up bathroom
- wrinkle-free, fully made beds
- all paperwork under control

Does the condition of your house support you and give you energy and joy? Or does seeing it and knowing all the energy it will take from you to live in it drag you down?

If you are visually oriented, draw a little floor plan, and perhaps sketch what you would like to create. Or collect magazine pictures that show how you'd like your home to look.

MAINTENANCE QUIZ

On a scale of 1 to 5 (1 being "This needs definite work," 5 being "We rock at this"), rate your ability to maintain organization in your house.

_____ I can welcome unexpected visitors without embarrassment most of the time.

_____ The kitchen is pretty well cleaned after meals and stays okay in between.

_____ The family is generally good at picking up after themselves.

_____ The family helps carry the overall load of housework to my satisfaction.

_____ Laundry (washing, drying, folding, putting away) is under control.

_____ Regarding bills, filing, magazines, etc., I have a paperwork system that works.

_____ Once I get an area organized, I generally keep it that way.

_____ The bathroom stays pretty much in order.

_____ The beds are made every morning.

_____ I can leave the house with a feeling of satisfaction about its condition.

A score of 10–19: Red Alert! You need to make maintenance a priority. Focus on specifics as you go through this section.

A score of 20–39: Code Orange! You have some aspects of maintenance under control, but there are areas that need work. It's tempting to say you are doing "good enough," but in reality you are only about halfway to having the kind of organized house you want.

A score of 40–50: Blue Ribbon! You are doing a stellar job of keeping your house organized. You and your family will not only have a house that is easier and more pleasant to live in, but being organized will open up wonderful areas in your life that will surprise you.

Look at the items you scored the poorest on. Based on your evaluation, give careful attention to the habits and systems that will make order happen for you in a consistent way.

This is the trip we're going to take—a journey to reach that imagined destination. Join us if you want to travel from chronic disorder—a place beyond dreams of what your life could be—to a permanent, new way of beautiful and organized living.

Ah! There Are Good Times Ahead

You want your house to be organized so you can come home without facing hours of work that you don't have the time or energy to do. You want it to look good. You want it to say "Welcome!" to you and your family and your friends. In addition, you want to be able to find things and work easily in the space you call home. And you don't want to have to work long hours to try to get and keep it organized, beautiful, and useful.

That's the practical side. But there's something that matters more. This is the soul of the matter: Deep down you know you were created for a different kind of life. A life of dignity, a life of service to others, a life of hospitality. Our hearts echo the words of legendary Notre Dame football coach Lou Holtz when asked how he overcame his negative beginnings: "I don't think God put us on this earth to be ordinary."[1] Deep down you feel—maybe you know—that God wants you to walk a victorious spiritual path that is being hindered because you haven't gotten your oh-so-earthly act together.

You've tried to do it by yourself in the past. You've vowed you are going to make it happen, and soon! You've bought books on organizing. In fact, they might form your biggest pile, if you could locate them all. Maybe you have even had partial success for a while. But trying to organize is like trying to lose weight or stop smoking. Sometimes you make progress and then slip back. Sometimes you get bogged down early in the game. Sometimes the progress is so slow, you get tired of working the plan you have. Your momentum fades away. This program addresses and overcomes these hindrances.

We Call It the Mount Rushmore Method

Now, if you are ready to quickly get your house in order with deep-down organizational changes that you can maintain, the program in this book is designed just for you. As we've already said, we call this powerful new approach the Mount Rushmore method, not to be confused with the Mount Vernon or Mount Vesuvius methods mentioned in our other books.

The "rush" indicates that the plan calls for the house to be cleared up quickly, in five days of activity. The "more" part of Rushmore indicates that it takes more than one person to execute this plan. Like the massive sculpture of four U.S. presidents, it requires a team.

You want your home to be different from what it is now—really, really different, right? Well, you can do it! You really can. Even if you have a long history of failures. Even if you have struggled for a long time, maybe years, without success.

Take our five-day challenge and be amazed at what happens. You've got everything to gain . . . and only a disorganized home to lose.

It's Hard to Change

This program is designed to get your house in order in only five days, and with minimal mental distress.

"How can I avoid distress?" you ask (because experiencing pain in the process is what has kept you from progress in the past). You do it by sidestepping that most-serious-of-all pain-producers: decision-making (groan!). You hate to make hard decisions about getting rid of things, about where to store things, about how to group things. You are a smart person, but when it comes to making simple decisions about how to handle your belongings, you crumble. It is your weak point, your own personal Kryptonite. The plan in this book cuts decision making to a minimum, while building support for you for the entire duration of your efforts. (We'll explain more about eliminating decisions and building support in the chapters ahead.)

> Even if you own a mansion, if you keep bringing things in and never throw anything away, eventually you will fill it up.

We understand your situation and how you feel about it. Both of us are among that wonderful group of people who have many good qualities, but staying effortlessly organized is definitely not one of them. We share certain characteristics that make organizing more troublesome for us than our neatnik neighbors, friends, and family, who seem to control their houses successfully with a minimum of effort. The difference is, we've learned what it takes to step out of the enforced confusion we used to live in. By applying what we have learned, we are able to enjoy the pleasures of coming home to an orderly environment, being able to retrieve what we need easily, and opening the front door to one and all on the spur of the moment. In this book, we'll share those secrets with you.

Fall in Love With an Organized Life

Real, long-term change will come only when the heart and mind passionately embrace the dream of an organized way of life, which fills our lives with what we really love—beauty. Many disorganized people actually have a keen love of beauty. That love spurs them to take home the charming figurine from the garage sale or to collect shiny marbles or coins. Sitting in their disordered homes, they proudly point out their lovely collections. Their shortsighted vision allows them to see the beauty in individual items, but their farsighted vision keeps them from noticing the wider view that illuminates the condition of the house as a whole. They love beauty but are too easily satisfied with individual items.

Somewhere along the way the fog begins to lift. Somewhere in the organizing process, they catch a glimpse that stirs a yearning for something beyond a messy house with touches of beauty. Messies all want more than a house that works well; we want it to look good, too. We know another way of life is possible. Pictures in magazines, memories of their childhood home, a visit to a friend's house or a model home, even television or movie settings remind them that it's desirable and possible. Their prime motivation begins to change to a love for what they can barely see at this time—a way of life full of charm and beauty.

Fall in love with order and beauty. Don't settle with living in a house whose condition drags you down, makes you sorry you have to live there. Do you wish you could just move to a fresh and lovely new house, leaving all you have behind? You can reinvent your house into that dream. Seek the happiness you will experience by getting the house under control and keeping it the way you dream it can be. You'll love it!

Getting It Under Control

1

The Clutterer Psyche

People like us, who struggle with clutter, have a much stronger attachment to our belongings than most. We see their possibilities, their beauty, and their place in our personal history with a special intensity. What is simple to others is complex to us. That's why we have more difficulty making decisions about what to do with the "treasures" that fill our homes.

Because most Messies are perfectionists at heart, whether our house looks like it or not, we feel just terrible if we make a "wrong" decision that we know we'll regret later. And we are more sensitive to the psychological pain that decision making brings. We say "I just can't" when it comes to letting go of a prized possession (and aren't they all prized?). We "awfulize" what might happen if we let it go and need it later. We are heartbroken if we feel we must part with something we love. No wonder we are sluggish when decision time comes around.

Many in the "orderly segment" of the population are not like that. In amazement, we watch our organized friends rip what we consider to be precious items out of their lives with hardly a twinge of care. They tolerate making mistakes—or just the possibility of making one—and move on. They don't seem to care if they will regret their decisions later. For them, it is not nearly as traumatic as it is for us. For whatever reason, we clutterers just get too emotionally attached to the things that come into our lives. Those organized people are able to continue life unscathed after getting rid of a belonging we would consider potentially useful or somewhat sentimental.

You need some of that calm approach from others who are organized. In the Mount Rushmore team approach of clearing the clutter from your home, only you will make final decisions about what to keep and what to let go. As the surfaces begin to clear, you'll see more realistically what you have, and how much you have of it.

As the project unfolds, you will realize that even though there are safeguards built into this Mount Rushmore approach, you're tapping in to the energy and efforts of others to help you overcome your natural tendency toward clutter. Using a carefully crafted plan, their skills can work wonders for your situation and still honor your desires about how you want to handle your belongings.

Clear Is Better Than Cluttered

We're on to something, right? There's something within you that yearns for relief from the chaos of disorganization. You don't like the way it looks, and you don't like the way it works. A few people who are way, way down at the end of the clutter scale continuum—the people we see on television shows about hoarding—seem insensitive to the seriousness of their situation. They are clutter-blind and frequently resist changing. But that is not you. You probably resonate with what Rhett Butler told Scarlet was his reason for leaving her chaotic life to seek peace in *Gone With the Wind*: "I want to see if somewhere there isn't something left in life of charm and grace." You know that the condition of your house is a big part of finding that charm and grace in your own life.

> "I want to see if somewhere there isn't something left in life of charm and grace."
> —Rhett Butler, *Gone With the Wind*

In a way, that "charm and grace" is hard to define. For many people, the condition of their house holds a spiritual aspect. They know that God is a God of order, and they suspect He values it in their lives. Some ask themselves, "What would Jesus do?" But Jesus didn't have a house or say anything about housekeeping. (Except maybe in the story of the woman who lost her money somewhere in the house. Now that rings a bell in our experience!)

Some fantasize for themselves or threaten their children with the question, "How would you feel if Jesus came to visit and saw your room like this, young lady!" Perhaps Jesus wouldn't appreciate being used as a threat for children to clean their rooms.

The Bible does say, "Whatsoever thy hand findeth to do, do it with thy might" (Ecclesiastes 9:10). And looking around the house, it may seem overwhelming for even the most willing heart to determine how to apply this verse.

Nonetheless, in spite of what may be confusion and inability on our parts, for many people, organization seems to be more than just making a mechanical improvement in our houses and lives for purely practical reasons. Something of who we are and why we were put on this earth seems to compel us to live differently. We know it's not right to live frustrated and hindered by an inability to keep the daily stuff of life under control. We want to tap in to the charm and grace Rhett Butler longed to experience, and which, we suspect, flows from a higher source. We want to live our best lives.

You Have Already Started

By picking up this book, you have demonstrated both the desire to change your house and the courage to consider an exciting plan that offers hope of real change. You are to be congratulated.

We know you'd love to find a quick and easy approach in executing the change. Well, this plan is as close to that as you will find. We're here to tell you that because of this unique approach, you will be able to move forward and have the stress-free house you want—one where you can function and are not ashamed of its condition. In short, by putting this plan into action, you can have what has eluded you for years!

Troy Produces His Own "Clean-up" Show

As an example of how this plan works, let's take a look at an extreme case that sets the pattern for us. Because of his home's excessive clutter, Troy, an accountant, hasn't invited anyone over in more than twenty years. During that time, whenever his elderly aunt came to town to visit, she would find accommodations in a hotel or with other relatives. But accommodating relatives had become scarce, and money for hotels had dried up. When she was ninety-three, Troy was forced to do the impossible—invite Auntie to stay with him.

When he learned his aunt was planning a visit, Troy flew into a massive cleanup effort, using every technique he'd learned in an organizing class. Some days he worked for twelve hours—sorting, putting things in boxes, throwing things out. Stuffing papers and debris into what grew to be a mountain of thirty-five boxes, he carved out some semblance of what each room should be. You could actually note which room was for dining, sleeping, food prep, etc. But time and his ability to handle the situation were nearly depleted . . . and the job was far from done.

His ninety-three-year-old aunt would arrive in six days, and the house was still a disaster. Even after his Herculean cleanup efforts to box and discard the things that were lying around, every surface in his home—tables, counters, chairs, cabinets, desk, dresser—still was piled high with ordinary things. Vying for every available inch were papers, batteries, cameras, cords, office supplies, tools, toiletries, and myriad other items best called "man stuff." Not by a long shot was the place good enough for Auntie.

What could be done to avert the shame he would feel if his aunt should see his situation? Troy considered the unthinkable—call in help from four friends with whom he had taken the organizing class. He knew they'd understand and would follow a plan for de-junking his place. So he quickly sent out a distress call.

With the team assembled, the plan was this: Each friend was positioned in a room with strict instructions to not throw anything away without first checking with Troy.

Each one's job was to sort into boxes the items in his assigned room based on the room where the item actually belonged. In addition, each person had a box labeled "Things I Think You Should Throw Away." Into that box would go all of the broken items and seemingly worthless things each helper would find. While his friends cleared and sorted, Troy's job would be to decide what to do with the broken and junky things recommended for the garbage pile.

LAMENT OF A SAVER

My Treasure Trove
I struggle to keep it all
day by day,
But as soon as I'm gone,
they'll toss it away.

At the end of an eleven-hour emergency marathon, they had filled twenty more boxes. Troy had discarded a truckload of broken and useless items. The original thirty-five boxes were stacked against a wall and attractively disguised with a decorative sheet. An additional twenty boxes were tucked into out-of-the-way spaces in rooms where their contents would finally be housed. With one grouping of boxes, the team even created a table by covering it with a decorative blanket Troy had acquired while traveling. By the end of the day, Troy's house was not only livable, it was beautiful.

In short, it was ready for Auntie.

Don't get us wrong. The house was not fully organized. But the boxes offered a good—albeit temporary—solution to his problem. Now Troy could operate from a clean perspective, emptying and organizing the things in each box one at a time, *after Auntie had gone.*

Troy's story, though it may not fit yours in its severity or detail, sets an example that fits our pattern of recovery. Troy had a keen desire to change, as you probably do. He had a long-standing problem that he'd tried to solve by himself without success. He called in outside help and, by using a plan we'll explain in more detail, he was able to reach his goal—and fast!

You can do it, too. By using the steps of the Mount Rushmore plan, adapted to your particular situation, you'll be able to reach your own personal goal so that you can function in the way you want and need to live. There's a whole new way of life right around the corner. No doubt about it.

It Will Be Worth It All

Each of us has a pressing reason to solve our clutter problem. By clearly identifying and giving words to your own personal motivation, you will validate and focus the change you want to make. Something has been irritating you for long enough that you now are saying, "Enough is enough!" Maybe several of these reasons apply to you:

- You are tired of seeing the clutter.
- You are embarrassed to let anyone come into your house.
- You waste time looking for things.
- You spend money buying duplicates for things you already have—somewhere.

- You have a specific emergency, such as a planned visitor.
- You don't want to leave this mess for your heirs.
- You need to move, but—oh, my!
- Your family is putting pressure on you to clean up.
- You feel helpless and hopeless because you can't solve the problem.
- You want beauty.
- The house is a continual burden.
- You are putting other things on hold until you solve this problem.

How many of these are your personal irritants? Each day they sap enthusiasm from your life. With each that can be eliminated or modified, your quality of life will improve, and it will be worth it.

After considering your motivations, write out a specific, tangible goal. Give it a date to create urgency. By _____, I want to accomplish _____.

By having a reason and giving it a deadline, you're on the way to achieving your goal! Your home will be in order, and you will finally be in full control of your life. The next chapter will open your eyes to a whole new way of looking at organizing, and will orient you on how to get started.

The System and the Team

The Winning Game Plan That Will Transform Your House

Your house may have been winning the clutter war up to this time, but now that you've identified the irritants that bother you most about it, you can use that awareness to gather motivation to mount a surprise offensive strike. Then watch the mess disappear! This approach has two basic parts:

- Assemble a team of workers whose time, effort, and energy will propel your progress with such speed that discouragement will not have time to set in.
- Clear all surfaces of clutter one day at a time using the human body as a guide—from foot to knee, from knee to shoulder, and from shoulder to the ceiling.

Using baby steps to do things slowly works for some situations, but sometimes it takes a bold move to jump-start the house out of chaos. If you follow the plan, it's guaranteed to have you blowing the trumpet of success and raising the flag of victory in record time, and with permanent results. Don't believe it? You will if you try it. We'll tell you how.

But Before You Move One Single Thing!

There is one very important question to consider before you begin: Where, exactly, do you want to put sorted items once they've been boxed and corralled? Along the walls? In the garage? In another storage area?

If you don't make this decision before you begin, you'll face a confusing, muddled mess during the project. But it doesn't have to be complicated. If you're running short on ideas, perhaps a friend could help you talk your way through this step.

One easy and effective way to make a good, workable plan is to draw a simple map of the layout of the house. Dimensions and scale are not important. Just a rough sketch of the floor plan will do nicely, as long as each room is included in its approximate position.

Once you've created that, write down what kinds of things belong in each room based on the "function" that you assign for each room. Most things are logical, but that doesn't mean you should skip noting it on the schematic.

For example, adult shoes can go to the master bedroom; misplaced dishes should be shuttled to the kitchen. Note those points on the map. But do you want the children's toys to go into their rooms, or into a corner of the dining room, or is there a rec room? Do you want the scattered books to find a permanent home on the bookshelf in the bedroom or the den? Create a general guide and label the floor plan, showing where each type of item should go.

Some things have no logical placement because they don't have a practical use. These might be memorabilia with sentimental value, or items given to us from people no longer alive. We feel that we should keep these items even though they have no obvious benefit for us: a large painting that doesn't really fit with the decor, a life-size suit of armor from the estate of a long-dead uncle, cassette tapes of all of Father's sermons, an extra microwave or non-working computer, a bag of feathers left over from a craft years ago. To move forward, you've got to select some spot for these types of things. Even if your choice is not perfect, any decision is better than none, and it's essential for you to make progress in your cleanup endeavor. You can always change later. Done is better than perfect.

Done is better than perfect.

Making these decisions ahead of time will give you and your helpers confidence later. You'll all have evidence despite the magnitude of the task at hand that things are under control and you have a plan worthy of enthusiasm. So do a little planning now. It will be worth it.

Explaining the Game Plan to Your Team

The Body's a Guide

It will be important to spark the enthusiasm of your helpers—an intriguing work plan can do the trick. So here it is:

You'll view your home as if it's a human body, focusing on one set of appendages per day. We'll explain in detail later. But just to give you a sneak peek now . . .

On Monday, you and your trusty team will clear the surfaces from the feet to the knees. Monday's work includes clearing clutter from the floor—the largest surface in the house—along with low bookshelves, tables, footstools, and other surfaces in the area from your feet to your knees. Take a moment right now to think about your low surfaces, and imagine them totally clear. No need to think about where the stuff will go; we'll worry about that later.

On Tuesday, you'll attack the region from knees to shoulders, clearing all surfaces, including tables, beds, bookshelves in that region, bathroom counters, toilet tops, and windowsills. You get the idea. (Seems like a big job? Don't worry. When the plan comes together, you'll see it works.) For now, just imagine it!

On Wednesday, you'll clear all surfaces from the shoulders to the top of the head. In this case, it includes to the ceiling. That region includes the refrigerator top, tops of bookcases, high shelves in the laundry room—anything that's been left untouched.

On Thursday, you'll tackle internal surfaces, such as cabinet and closet shelves, the insides of bathroom vanities, drawers, etc. At this point, the house will have made a U-turn and you'll be able to concentrate on creating order.

On Friday, you and your team will venture beyond the working areas of the house to the storage areas, attacking surfaces in the attic, utility room, and/or garage.

By Saturday, your project will be done, or "done enough," and it will be time to celebrate! You should be at a stopping point, and your house should be much improved from where it was when you began. Sure, you'll need to go back and address the things in the boxes neatly stacked in various rooms. But at that point, it will be time to take a breath, appreciate what you've done, and begin to build on your new foundation of order. You will undoubtedly want to add cleanliness, beauty, and fun after things are clear.

In section 2 of this book, we'll plan and give you some advice and helpful hints for going through the boxes and creating a place for everything that should remain in your home. But now it will be reward time for you and your team. If you have thought ahead and planned for it, you could throw a party at your "new" house that weekend. If you are plumb tuckered out, you may just want to set a time for the gang to get together for a back-slappin', cleaned-house hoedown celebration!

Remember that on each of these workdays, you'll follow the same basic plan. Everybody in his or her zone will start with six storage boxes. Add more boxes if needed. They can be purchased inexpensively in flattened multipacks from big-box superstores, office-supply stores, or home-improvement warehouses. Economy quality will be fine for your needs.

Your helpers will be able to assemble them easily following the directions printed on each box. And as they work, sorting items cluttering your home into groups of similar items, they'll label the outside of each box according to what's in it, where the items were found, and where they need to go. The labels on the boxes may look something like these: "Papers From the Family Room to the Office," "Kitchen Items From the Family Room," "Toys From the Family Room to the Kids' Rooms,"

"Pet Items From the Family Room to the Garage," "Shoes From the Family Room," "Clothing From the Family Room to the Bedroom Closet." One box will be labeled "Trash."

Working only on the region of the day, helpers will sort things from each area into the appropriate box. When a box is filled, the team member will construct another one and put it on top of the first, labeling it appropriately.

At the end of each day's sorting work, the boxes will be deposited in the appropriate rooms, lined up neatly against the walls, or wherever you've designated. White boxes with neat labels will be much more pleasing to the eye than a hodgepodge of cast-off boxes of various sizes and hues. The value of using this neat approach can't be overstated. See how it all works by reading about the success that Roberta and her friends had in bringing her clutter under control.

Roberta and Friends Dive In

Anita and Roberta were part of a loose-knit garden club made up of women in their neighborhood. After the discussion about gardening, the conversation rolled around to house-keeping. When Roberta expressed her frustration with the condition of her house, Anita was quick to offer help, and a few of the others chimed in to volunteer, too. It seemed like a fun thing to do.

Anita was excited about helping her neighbor. She loved helping others, and organizing was her strong point. But when she got to Roberta's house, she was truly surprised at the mess she saw. She had heard about really messy household situations, but this was far beyond what she'd imagined they would find. Items from everywhere were strewn all over the house.

With compassion and a desire to "make it right," she tackled her zone, the den. Using her six boxes, she came up with categories that fit what she saw. She labeled the boxes of papers from the den, adding specifics about where she'd found them in the den. Her boxes read, "Papers From Desk," "Papers From Table," and "Papers From Den Floor."

She labeled other boxes "School Supplies From Den," "Clothes From Den," "Books From Den," and "Trash." As she worked, she could see that it would be important later to have information about not only what was in each box, but also the room in which it had been collected and the room where it all belonged. This would help Roberta later when she began to unpack each box.

Soon, Anita found she needed additional boxes, because often similar items were destined for different rooms. For instance, children's shoes went in a box headed for their rooms. Adult shoes went in a separate box destined for the master bedroom. One item at a time, she happily cleared the floor, footstools, and other low surfaces. Organizing was soothing to her, and she looked forward to returning the next day to work on the area from knees to shoulder.

Another member of the team, Jose, chose to work in the office because of his love for books—and there were plenty of them there. He fulfilled his obligation for that day but chose not to return because, although he loved to read books, he didn't like to shuffle them. The repetition bored him. For him, the task was not a good fit, and that's okay. So someone else took his assignment.

At the end of each day, the boxes were carted to the rooms where those items ultimately belonged. Boxes of clothes and shoes went to the bedroom, papers to the office, utensils and foodstuffs to the kitchen, toys to the kids' rooms, etc. It didn't always go smoothly, but with careful direction each day, more and more was cleared away, until the out-of-place contents of the whole house had been sorted into labeled boxes and stacked in the appropriate rooms. All surfaces were clear. Now Roberta could do the final sorting and placement.

At first Roberta was very skeptical about putting her papers in boxes. Although they were strewn about the house in every conceivable space—on tables, on shelves, and in all of the nooks and crannies—she still held on to the idea that she knew where everything was. She went to sleep after the first day of work a little wary. *What if I forget about something?* she thought.

> "Coming together is a beginning. Keeping together is progress. Working together is success."
> —Henry Ford

Sure enough, at 4 a.m. she bolted awake. "The Thompson report!" She'd left in on the third pile on the left side of the credenza, a third of the way down, on top of the concert flyer. Convinced it would be lost forever, she got up, put on her slippers and robe, and regretfully padded down toward the credenza area.

The credenza had been cleared! Yikes! Now what? She began looking at box labels and saw the box labeled "Papers From the Left Side of the Credenza." She couldn't believe it! She opened the box and, sure enough, the papers she had in the stack on the left side of the credenza were there, all accounted for, in the same order they were in when they sat on the credenza.

Roberta thumbed a third of the way down, and . . . there was the Thompson report. Whew! She snatched it up and took it with her to her bedroom.

The next morning, bright and early, Roberta jumped out of bed. She smiled as she looked around her neat-and-clean, box-lined home, and thought, *I really do know where everything is!*

Plan Work Before You Work Your Plan

Knowing how to work the plan is not the same as planning. The natural desire for most of us is to jump in immediately and start moving things around. This was the case with Julia.

When her team walked in on their first day, she was raring to go and started shuffling clutter from one place to the next, encouraging the team members to join in. She was disappointed when the team leader held back and said they needed more direction than just "start cleaning up." Clear focus and communication are the bedrocks of a good beginning. Julia needed to orient herself to the task before them. Otherwise she would not be able to clearly evaluate whether the goals for that day had been met.

> *Team* means **T**ogether **E**veryone **A**chieves **M**ore!

It was then that Julia realized that she really did need to decide on answers to these questions before beginning:

- What do we want to accomplish today? (Since it was the first day, she knew the plan was to do all surfaces from floor to knee.)

- If we could only accomplish one thing today, what would be the most important?
- What is the second-most important thing we accomplish?
- The third?

After thinking through her answers and prioritizing what she really wanted to get done, Julia smiled. She wanted the floor to be clear; she wanted them to keep an eye out for her missing watch with the gold band—a gift from her grandmother; and she wanted her papers to be stacked neatly. Finally, if there was a little time at the end, she thought it would be nice to vacuum the rug a little. And after she explained it to them, her team members seemed to understand clearly. Now they, too, were enthusiastic to begin. *Yes,* she thought. *Today will be a most productive day!*

Julia vowed to focus on those goals to help avoid unrealistic expectations. She didn't want to be disappointed at the end of that first day if the house wasn't cleared as much as she'd dreamed.

Just like Julia, you also need to keep in mind that even though the floor and low surfaces will be cleared, the house will still have a disheveled look and some things will have been moved from their regular places. You likely will feel some discomfort about that. The feeling of disorder in the house could get worse before it gets better, but it *will* get better. It helps to keep that thought in mind.

But before you start leading your team, it's important for you to have some clear goals and procedures in mind. It will help for you to prepare an instruction sheet to each member of your team. Every team is more successful when they are

Our Game Plan

1. Starting with about six assembled boxes per person, sort items from today's surface into the boxes provided, grouping like items headed to the same destination.
2. With a marker, neatly label the box, indicating the room the items came from and the room they belong in. (Example: "Shoes From Living Room for Master Bedroom," "Toys From Living Room for Kids' Room," "Books From Bathroom for Bookshelf," "Papers From Kitchen for Office," etc.) Bills or important-looking papers should go in a special box.

   Some categories will be:
   Papers (general)
   Bills or papers that look important
   Shoes
   Clothing
   Toys
   Pets
   Books
   Electronics
2. Don't throw away anything. Put possible throw-away items into a box labeled "Trash" to be handled later by the owner or team leader. Talk to the team leader about any questionable items. The reason this program works is because the homeowner makes *all* of the final decisions. Your job today is to help by sorting and boxing items.
3. Continue until the surface you are working on is completely clear. Once a surface is clear, it would help if you would remove dust and dirt from the surface by vacuuming, dusting, polishing, etc. But this cleaning is optional.
4. Put back any items that belong on that surface, such as a telephone or important photo. If you are not sure, consult the team leader.
5. Leave boxes stacked neatly against the wall in the room where the items ultimately belong.
6. And remember: The rule is once a surface is clear, NOTHING— and that means NO (inappropriate) THING—should go back there!

Stick to the five-day plan—that way our effort will work better and will be more fun for everybody.

Thank you!

following the same game plan. This kind of project is unique and requires careful orientation.

Give copies of your instruction sheet to every member of the team at your first "huddle" when you gather on Day One, or perhaps at an informal meeting at your home the day before you begin.

Where Seldom Is Heard a Discouraging Word

Project Do's and Don'ts

Avoid unexpected problems by reminding yourself and your team of the following guidelines. Experience has shown they're important to keep in mind.

GUIDELINES FOR THE HOMEOWNER/TEAM LEADER

Do's

1. Appreciate and thank each of these wonderful people.
2. Appreciate their courage to start a new job, and understand that they have come to help you.
3. Maintain a cheerful disposition—remember that your team members are here to make you happy. Your attitude matters!

Don'ts

1. Don't focus on details of how your team is working. Keep the big picture in mind. Let them do their job.
2. Don't practice perfectionism. Realize that you may be a perfectionist, but they may not be. Be flexible.
3. Don't ask the team members to do housework or maintenance work for you. They are here to help you get surfaces clear. Stay focused on the goal!

Guidelines for the Team Members

Do's

1. Show respect for the owner as a person and their courage in inviting you in.
2. Have a cheerful, encouraging attitude, and remain positive during the time you are at the person's home.
3. Include the owner in any side conversations about her possessions.
4. Be sensitive! Remember that this may be very hard for the person you are there to help.
5. Maintain strict confidentiality. Guard the privacy of the homeowner. What happens in the house stays in the house.

Don'ts

1. Don't comment on the condition of the house or make inappropriate facial expressions. Be careful of what you say.
2. Refrain from giving ANY advice about anything unless asked (other than, possibly, safety precautions).
3. Don't throw anything away or give advice to the owner about throwing things away.

Thoughts to Move You Forward

On Your Mark—Get your attitude adjusted and your enthusiasm bubbling. Overcome the inertia of discouragement. Fan the small spark of hope that helps you believe that this time the outcome really *will* be different. This time you will finish the job and begin living life unencumbered by confusion and clutter.

It takes courage to step up to the starting line one more time. It takes courage to face change—even change for the better. It takes courage to reach out to others and form a team. But here you are, contemplating doing just that. You're on the mark, ready to go.

Get Set—Now it's time to get your gear ready. Assemble the supplies you need and select helpers for your team. List possible candidates. Then pick up the phone and call. Ask people to join your team. You'll be amazed at what happens when you reach out for help.

You've seen the reality shows, the ones where a team cleans up and re-creates a home. Well, it's that team approach that's a key element in making this plan incredibly successful.

If you think you can't create a team, or if the idea of sharing the task with others makes you shudder, don't despair. Though we strongly urge you to gather a group of helpers, and we'll tell you how to do it, the technique outlined in this book also can work for a team of one. Of course, by working with a team, you'll get the job done more quickly and probably with better success. We'll show you how to do it . . . and have a good time, too. Remember this motto: You alone can do it, but it's easier if you don't do it alone.

Go—The unique key element of the Mount Rushmore plan is that the specific focus is on clearing surfaces of the house. That will be our mantra, our battle cry: Clear the surfaces! Clear the surfaces! Clear the surfaces!

YOUR GO-TO GEAR—To prepare for Day One, you'll need these supplies ready and set aside:
- White storage boxes, one package of ten for each volunteer. Approximate cost: $16 per team member. You can return any unopened packages you don't need.
- Transparent tape and/or sticky notes
- Black markers (broad point is best for visibility)
- Printed instructions for team members
- Snack food, such as chips, nuts, maybe some fruit, so the team can nibble and keep working
- Lots of water
- Cups
- Napkins
- A cheerful attitude

Choose the week you'll set aside to transform your house. Coordinate with your team, put them on the starting line, and move forward toward the finish. Can't you just hear the cheering crowds as you cross the line!

Now's the time to take some "before" shots with a camera so you—and your team members—can truly enjoy the before-and-after comparison, maybe at a post-project party to celebrate your success. The next chapter gets to the heart of the game plan.

3

Getting Down to Business

Karen's Freedom From Her "Horribly Messy Basement"

Karen finally was ready to admit it. Her 1,500-square-foot unfinished basement was a huge mess. She was willing to part with many of the items stored there, but she felt she just couldn't tackle such a big job on her own.

Many of the items had been inherited: She'd accumulated things after her grandmother died, and again when her in-laws passed. With three small children, she also had a growing collection of toys and clothes they'd outgrown. She just didn't know what to do with it all.

Her dad had offered to finish part of the basement, transforming it into a family room, a couple of closets, an office, and a bathroom. The window of time when he could work on it was quickly approaching. She'd committed to clearing out the half that would incorporate the project, but her husband and father were beginning to voice their doubts about whether she could really do it. Karen took that as a challenge and vowed she would not fail.

She was in a moms' group at the time, and they gave her encouragement, telling her that cleaning out her basement was both possible and reasonable. They also said they would help. The cavalry was coming! In just three weeks, a trio of volunteers would arrive to help with the big project.

Alternately thrilled and apprehensive, Karen went right to work trying to at least tidy up. She made some immediate progress, recycling a pile of old newspapers here, and rearranging a few areas to quickly make it look neater there. Part of Karen's planning for success also involved making arrangements for her husband and young children to be away while she and her team were working in the basement. That eliminated distraction and allowed her to focus on her task.

On the appointed Saturday, three women from the group arrived and headed down to the basement. Because they weren't close friends, Karen didn't feel quite as concerned about what they might be feeling about her mess. The rules were that they would ask her about *everything* and help her clear out the area that was to be the construction zone.

At first the women chose way too many categories, like Bedroom, Family Room, Filing, Goodwill, Church, etc. This started becoming unwieldy, and Karen was having difficulty making decisions. Finally, Karen gently asked if they could make the categories broader so she would have fewer choices to make.

They chose three categories for sorting: "Keep," "Garage Sale," and "Trash." Fortunately, Karen had removed much of the trash during her prep work in the previous three weeks.

Within a few hours, the women had created a mountain of garage sale items. Each helper took home some items she really liked. That made Karen feel good—like the women's volunteer efforts had paid off for them, too.

Karen enjoyed finding homes for the various items she'd decided to give away. She gave more away to friends, then held a garage sale within a few days.

Best of all, her formerly messy basement was ready to be transformed into a beautiful, useful area of her home . . . all thanks to a speedy team effort.

Some of the items had landed in the basement for long-term storage. Other items would be put to use when the new rooms were available. Part of her team's effort was to ensure that furniture to be used in the new family room wouldn't be trapped behind items packed in a corner for long-term storage.

> "It was so nice to have the extra hands and minds to free me from the feeling of being overwhelmed and not knowing where to start."

"It was so nice to have the extra hands and minds to free me from the feeling of being overwhelmed and not knowing where to start," Karen recalled. "They just dug right in, and I started making the decisions while they moved things. It was exhausting. But when we were done, it was amazing to see the space we'd created!"

"It's hard to de-clutter all at once," she admitted. "I did it in stages. The first and biggest stage was when I went through the basement with the three women."

After she was off to such a great start, she planned a garage sale every year and tackled yet another area of the remaining clutter on her own. Some of the items lasted through a few rounds of decision making before she was ready to part with them.

"It's a freeing process to let things go . . . but only when you're *ready* to let them go," Karen said. "Often, for me, it's a matter of being realistic. Do I really think I'm going to use a particular item? Sometimes it takes a few years of asking that question until I realize it's not worth storing the item one more season, since I haven't used it and likely won't. I realized that I wanted to be able to use the basement space much more than I wanted to keep the things that were creating the mess.

"For me, having the team come to my home was a turning point, and I have not been back to the place where I just bring things in without thinking of the bigger picture. My kids remember the full basement where there was just an aisle to the laundry area and furnace with no place to play. When they get into the mode where they want to keep every little thing, I remind them that if they try to keep everything, their houses will end up looking like our basement did, and worse!"

Since her basement-clearing adventure began, Karen's been able to clear enough of an area to finish another large area of the basement, making it into a bedroom. Now she hopes to transform the laundry area and finish the remaining section as an exercise/game room. Go, Karen!

A "Party Girl" Opens Her Doors

Teams have been the backbone of successful ventures since man and womankind started tackling projects too big for one. One of the examples most familiar to us is how rural farmers of a community used to gather to help a neighbor build a barn. The Amish and a few other groups still do. Smart people!

They have a plan to follow. They have leadership. They have support from another team—the womenfolk—who fix great meals to keep them fed and hydrated along the way. Most of all they have fun along with a sense of having accomplished something important. They do it all with a feeling that they belong to a community. Working in teams has a long and stellar history, and you can harness its power, too.

Dawn always brought life to the many organizations to which she belonged. Her church friends and fellow choir members were especially important parts of her social network. She loved them and they loved her. A few knew why they were never invited to her house. Most didn't.

When she got hold of the team-cleaning idea, she loved it, because it sounded

Many hands make light work.

a little like having a party with a purpose. As she thought about it further, though, she began to hesitate about whom she would invite. Richard was neat but a little critical. She definitely didn't want anybody who might be judgmental. Karen sometimes brought two purses to church to be sure she had what she needed. Maybe she was too disorganized. Her good friend Brenda had two older kids and a new baby. She for sure wouldn't have time to help.

After careful thought, she finally settled on a handful of people to ask, and to her delight, four out of the five accepted her invitation—four people she knew could help without judging her.

She was right; they were great. And when the week was done, she invited a large group of friends to her celebration party to honor her team members and have that party she'd never been able to have before. When she explained the process for the work the team had done, to her surprise, several others wanted to develop their own teams to come to their houses for an on-the-double pickup project.

Assembling Your Team

If you are unsure about being in charge when your team is at work, have someone like an advisor or capable friend there to help you. Perhaps that person can help you find suitable team members to start with. Be sure to select someone who won't make you feel uncomfortable or judged and will help you manage having so many people in your home at once.

Rightly done, getting a team to work together on your house can be an uplifting experience for you and the friends who join you on your journey to an organized home. They may like it so much, they'll want a team to come to their houses for this same procedure. They may even set up a service or ministry using this five-day plan so they can help others in the same way they're helping you.

Something that every owner in professional sports knows is that putting together a great team is perhaps the most important factor in determining whether it will be a winning season.

When it comes to choosing your team, it's important to remember that not everybody will make an effective team member. There is no shame in that. The important thing is to find those who can get the job done with commitment and enthusiasm.

For you, close friends might be the best team members. But some people feel more comfortable working alongside people with whom they're not as close. Some find that a family team works just fine. For others, that would be a disaster. Ideally, the size of the team should match the size of the house and, to a certain extent, the conditions of the surfaces.

> Every endeavor can be reduced to three elements:
>
> • Good People
> • Good Project
> • Good Plan
>
> Without the first one, you can't do much with the other two.

How large should your team be? If you have enough people, two per room seems to work nicely for support and camaraderie. It also acts as a check and balance. And if you have enough help, choose someone to act as a floater to take things into the correct rooms and to bring around extra supplies if needed. Of course, any team may have some issues they will have to work through. Be flexible in your decisions to fit your situation.

But your best bets may be people who have:

- *Time*—This is a busy world. Choose team members who will be able to see you through to the end of the project.
- *Energy*—This is not heavy work (usually), but it requires physical movement all the way through.
- *Enthusiasm*—Do they like to help others? Maybe they particularly want to help you. Will they feel proud of what they have done when the job is finished?

- *Cooperative spirit*—Your decisions rule. Will they commit to the game plan you set without interjecting their own?
- *Pleasantness*—The team has a strong social component. Do the team members get along? Will they have fun doing the job together?

For this job, it will be best to avoid asking for help from someone with whom you often disagree. If that person wants to be included, perhaps he or she can run errands or help prepare for the celebration at the end of the five-day process.

Evaluate prospective team members by asking yourself:

- Will this person be accepting about the condition of my home?
- Do I feel comfortable about having him or her on my team?
- Will this person follow the rules about sorting?

For suggestions about where to find team members, check out the resources in the appendix at the back of the book.

Making the Invitation

An organizing team is probably a new concept for many people, and working on an organizing team will likely be a new idea to those you are going to invite to help you. You need to have an encouraging explanation ready. Do it using an invitation.

First you'll need to decide on a time for your project. Maybe you envision the group meeting on consecutive weekdays, as

HELP! I NEED YOU!

I've got a fun, unique experimental project planned, and you're invited to join me.

WHAT'S THE GOAL? Totally refreshing, de-cluttering, and upgrading in a home organization project in just five days. In short, doing an extreme makeover, moving from topsy-turvy to totally transformed. Like a do-it-yourself television makeover!

HOW WILL WE ACCOMPLISH THIS? Using a team and a unique approach. You're invited to be a part of the team. "Together we are better" is our mantra.

WHEN WILL THE TEAM MEET TO DO THIS FUN PROJECT? _____

HOW MUCH TIME WILL IT TAKE? As much or as little time as you can commit to, but in five days we are closing up shop.

WHAT TO WEAR?
- comfortable shoes
- casual clothes
- a positive attitude punctuated with a smile

WHAT'S YOUR REWARD? As a team member, you will probably be surprised at how exciting and satisfying the work will be. It's hard to understand until you've experienced it. The payoff is that you get to be part of this wonderful transformation. Even better, you will be with friends—sort of a fun party with a purpose. And who knows, maybe you'll want the team to come to your house next!

When the task is accomplished, we'll have a team celebration party. Hope you can come! Please let me know.

designed in this program, so you have a new house in five days. Or you can adjust it to a once-a-week meeting. If your house needs less work, you might be able to zip through all five days of tasks in just two days. Try to find a time that's likely to work for everybody so you can keep the team together for the synergy it will create. If this isn't possible, you can also have team members come and work at different times.

Maybe you would want to make an invitation designed something like the one on page 59.

Team Idea "Works Wonderfully"

Marina writes about her "amazing" experience with having a group over for a day to help her organize:

> I had a team of girl friends come over and help for a day. I think it is a great idea and works wonderfully. I wish we would work together more often; we could accomplish more with each other. However, the synergistic effect and doing things with friends is amazing. It may not be for everyone, but it has helped me.

Making the Goals Clear—Speed Is the Need

When your friends hear what's brewing, questions will bubble up quickly. Now is when you harness their enthusiasm. Explain that at the end of the week, all the surfaces of your house from top to bottom will be clear. No junk, no clutter, no embarrassment when visitors come, no discouraging mess when you come home. Your house will radiate a neat and orderly appearance. Period! But without a team, none of this wonderful stuff will happen.

A secondary goal is that you can easily maintain it after the team goes home.

We'll talk about how to do that in section 2.

A clear and focused goal is the secret of team success. For the five-day, total-house project, it's crucial for you and your team to keep three goals in mind:

1. Clear the surfaces.
2. Clear the surfaces.
3. Clear the surfaces.

And you don't just want to clear them. You need to clear them fast.

Welcome to the Wonderful Team

When the day arrives and the team members walk through the door, either en masse or individually, you'll want to welcome them and orient them to the plan mentioned in chapter 2.

Show the supplies and explain the Mount Rushmore plan. Let them know they will be working on a five-day basis using the idea of "body" as an organizational guide, setting the order of work for the surfaces to be cleared. Divvy up the various areas.

> "Alone we can do so little; together we can do so much."
> —Helen Keller

Show them where the rest rooms and refreshments are located. Answer questions. Then, without further ado, let them scurry off to their posts to get started.

As you plan, you'll want to remember to do everything you can to diminish the desire to dawdle. Aim to get your team on board with the five-day (and five-day only) plan, rather than allowing the mission to spread out over a longer period. Speed is the need . . . and here's why: When you have clear spaces all over the house, they carry a power of their own toward helping maintain orderliness. There is something heartening about having cleared surfaces. Most people resist breaking the beauty barrier created by a shining surface. It keeps them from allowing clutter to pile up there again, and inspires them to do the proper maintenance needed to keep it clear.

If you get some parts of the house organized and leave other parts junky, the junky areas visually pollute the neat areas. Debris tends to drift into clear areas. Soon you're right back to Clutterdom.

**Speed
is the need.**

Communicate the need for working quickly to your team members by putting up signs saying *Speed is the need.* Don't distract them by talking to them or stopping them for some other reason. If they drift off task, nicely remind them of time constraints.

And when *you* feel like slowing down, focus your attention on the payoff of your accomplishments: the joy of having a house that looks good and works well, and the ability to enjoy friends in your home without embarrassment and without having to work so hard to prepare to invite them in. You'll celebrate all of this at the victory party when you're done at the end of five days.

Kim's Story—Her Goals and Team

Kim from Australia had an interesting experience. Things had gotten way out of control. Counters were covered with mail and random papers, chairs were littered with clothing, her kitchen and laundry room were messy with things scattered about. It seemed there was nowhere to just sit and relax, and she felt she could no longer enjoy her home. Tearfully, Kim admitted she could not do the organizational job required all by herself. She had been trying but was just overwhelmed. She needed to bring in support. Her solution—she asked a friend to come over to help her de-clutter her messy house.

> This book is designed to accomplish one end—at the end of the week, all surfaces of your house, from top to bottom, will be clear. And they'll stay that way.

Somewhere along the way, the friend gathered a few more friends. And before long, they had an impromptu team. Although Kim had hesitated to start, and didn't have a real goal when she first began, as her growing team began to work, she better formulated both the goal and her plan. The team members' calm detachment and matter-of-fact, confident attitudes helped Kim make decisions. Their teamwork got the job done. And when the job was finished, she ended up feeling, in her words, "liberated."

Her final words were "Do whatever works to get your stuff under control."

Cheryl Needed That All-Important Game Plan

Cheryl from South Texas knew she wanted to tackle her clutter using the team approach. And she had willing workers.

The problem, she admitted afterward, was that she didn't have a plan. When she wrote to tell us about her experience, she had this to report:

> Very sweet and wonderful friends from my life group at church wanted very badly to help me with this part of my life that has dragged me down for years upon years. They came with grungy clothes, work gloves, cleansers, lawn chairs, a cooler full of ice, and chilled bottled water.
>
> The women came into my small duplex and set right to work sweeping the floor, washing dishes, gathering boxes. The men were outside cleaning my carport—thoroughly cleaning it. They even got the rusty door open to let some air in. One guy hauled several truckloads of trash and broken furniture to the Dumpster at his business. It was a great day of fellowship. And being that I don't have much money—and they assured me they didn't want any—I thanked them with coupons for ice cream.

But later, Cheryl realized how the end result could have been even more effective.

> While it was a wonderful day and an awesome gesture on their part, and a risk on my own part for letting people into this dark and messy side of me, the group cleaned like a group would. It looked a lot more organized. They had asked me for a game plan at the start, but the precise problem was that I didn't have one. "Important stuff and unimportant stuff got boxed together and stacked neatly in the carport for me to go through slowly and bring back into the house when ready.
>
> They worked hard that day. It was a very giving and loving and blessed thing they did for me. I just regret that I did not

have a game plan. A game plan would have been the thing to have.

Donna and Tracy—Two Different, Yet Successful, Experiences

Every time Donna walked into her home she felt demoralized. It seemed everywhere she looked there was clutter, and it left her feeling tired and defeated. Now, due to circumstances beyond her control, it had fallen to her to host parties for three big high school family graduations approaching. She definitely was not prepared.

There would be family from out of town, plus the kids and their families, whom she had never met. Why had she let it get so cluttered! Desperation led her to take a bold step. She overcame the mixed feelings that flooded in when she asked for help from her sisters in transforming her home. Thankfully, they agreed. In telling the story, she wrote: "My two sisters came into my house to get ready for our three kids' high school graduations. My feelings ranged from intimidation, anger, joy, frustration, and relief."

And they did the job—using their own version of a team approach. During the process, they got rid of some things Donna would have kept,

> "I kept going because I wanted it done for the parties."

but she kept her eye on the final goal. "I worried about wasting things, because they aren't as frugal as I am. I did have a feeling of loss of control, but I kept going because I wanted it done for the parties."

The parties were great. The kids were grateful. The family and friends could not have enjoyed the parties more. She wouldn't have missed it for the world. Years later they would remember the year of the parties at Donna's house.

Tracy's experience was very different. She didn't believe it was possible to get her house under control. In caring for two young children and a husband, she was completely frustrated and overwhelmed with the duties of maintaining her home.

"It's important to get meals done on time, help the children with their homework, and create a pleasant home for my husband—and I'm a failure because I can never get these things done!" Tracy lamented. "I feel guilty every day. Why can't I get anything done?"

Tracy finally realized that her problem was a lack of time management, which led to massive amounts of clutter landing everywhere in her home. After sitting down and creating a schedule for herself—one requiring that she work on her organizing for two hours every morning, and allowing herself freedom every day after noon—she finally had the time to create the home she so desperately wanted for her family.

Realizing that "within structure there is freedom," Tracy created the time. Now all she needed was a plan.

"I tried to get a team together, but nobody was available during the day," she recalled. "And I didn't want to try to clean and organize when my family was home, so I just did it myself."

Every day Tracy worked the plan and became the team. Just like the Mount Rushmore method goes, Monday was her floor-to-knees day; Tuesday was knees-to-shoulders day;

on Wednesday she worked from shoulders to the ceiling; on Thursday she worked on interior surfaces; and on Friday she worked on storage units.

Because she was working alone, it took significantly longer. But by committing to consistency, she finally triumphed. She applied the maintenance habits you'll find in the second section of the book, and her home stayed beautifully, comfortably organized.

Here was the important thing for Tracy: "The plan didn't interfere with my family. As a matter of fact, it gave me more freedom to care for my family and stop neglecting my friends."

Using the plan we describe here, Tracy was able to get her home organized and still have time for her family. She even started a brand-new career—she's now a successful professional organizer!

Tracy is happy, and you can be, too! This book gives you a plan that will work. All you have to do is make the time to work it.

If you must be a group of one because you can't develop a team, you can still use many of the ideas presented here, such as

- Make a plan before you begin.
- Sort into boxes by where things *should* be.
- Be sure to label each box.
- At the end of the day, place the boxes in the correct rooms.

By making it into a kind of game, you will feel less isolated, and this will help to push you out of the same old rut that's not getting you anywhere near your goal.

Attitude Is Everything

Deep down, you may feel there's little hope that you'll ever really change the condition of your home and capture the joy of living a clutter-free, even organized, life. But take heart: Just by reading this book, you've taken a critical step on the path to progress. Really! Being willing to try is the first step in change.

Maybe you can relate to the following people, who desperately wanted a different life:

Brenda wrote to us and lamented, "I have piles of paper, books, and miscellaneous items all over my house, waiting to go to their designated spots (not to mention the dust and dog hair). Problem is, there is no designated spot, and the piles just sit there. My house is a disaster."

Renee wrote in despair, "No matter how much I try to get everything all clean and organized, more stuff keeps coming and coming and coming! Some days I want to give up, but then I realize that other people have the same size house, the same number of children, and basically the same life as I do. It makes me wonder what's wrong with me. Frankly, I think I'm beyond help."

Carlos admitted, "I organized for twelve hours and threw out fourteen bags of trash, yet it looks like I haven't done a thing!"

If this is your situation, can you really make a change? You betcha! And you will—we promise. But you have to follow through on the Mount Rushmore plan, then follow up with maintenance tips we'll provide starting in chapter 6. But first you need to find the key that will make your efforts work this time. That key is you or, more specifically, your attitude and way of thinking.

Attitude is everything. Florence, one of the mentors in the Messies Anonymous website support group, expressed during a telechat that the most important thing for her was a change in the way she looked at things. It was an attitude situation. For many years she felt she could not go fast enough to accomplish everything, so she did nothing. She did not have the time or energy. The mess just grew and grew. She felt there was no way she could win.

Then Florence adopted the attitude that, no matter what it took, she was not going to continue to live with wall-to-wall debris in her huge three-story Victorian home. This new resolve was her turning point. Because she was determined to win the battle against clutter, she was willing to, as she calls it, "participate." Participate she did, putting full effort into a total cleanup. And now, in that house in which there was once nothing to make her smile, she is smiling all day.

That same steely resolve will spur you on to doing what it takes to make the change you cannot live without, to solidify your vision, to gather your team. In short, to get the job done. The next chapter deals with the details of each of the five days of the Mount Rushmore plan.

Putting the Plan Into Action

Before anyone arrived, Marjorie set out the supplies, snacks, and drinks she'd gathered earlier. Then she made a list of items that were to be set aside for charity or a garage sale, and she also made a list of things she hadn't been able to find: a missing ring, her Christmas gift list, and a special information-packed notebook. When team members arrived, she asked them to be on the lookout for these items as they worked. It might be a good idea to collect any valuables such as important keys, money, jewelry, and any other items you want to keep secure, and store them away in a safe place. Marjorie then designated spaces to group items that were too large to fit into the white boxes.

Remember, as Marjorie did, you will have the final word. You won't feel comfortable if you feel out of control. Marjorie thought of the job like a game and envisioned herself as the team coach. That made the process feel less stressful.

Think of yourself in that way, as well. You are the leader of a valuable group of people with a significant goal. But resolve not to micromanage. Give team members freedom to play their positions.

You may decide to turn over the coordination efforts to someone else so you can direct your attention to unexpected things that come up. You're probably not a naturally well-organized person. Your "subcontractor" probably should be.

Some people are naturals or have developed what is called, in the organizing world, "executive function." They are good at planning, controlling their urges, initiating a task, and maintaining focus. They are able to see the scope and sequence of a project clearly.

> **The reason this plan will absolutely work is because it does not require team members to make any significant decisions.**

Visualizing the overall concept from the beginning to the end is the scope. Seeing the steps it takes to get the job done quickly and easily is the sequence. For example, at the end of the first day, all surfaces from the knees to the floor will be cleared. That is the goal. The steps to reach that goal involve allowing team members to put things into boxes to be taken to the room where they ultimately belong. The next step will be to empty the boxes on your own, after the team has done its work. The person with executive function can keep this whole process on track.

Though we can, and should, work on developing executive function, it just doesn't come naturally to most of us who are disorganized by nature. Fortunately, most of us know people who are strong in that area, and we can pull together on special projects. But if you want to retain control of the five-day transformation project in your home, this book provides the goals and steps set out in orderly fashion.

"Magic" White Boxes Are the Key

When your team starts to work, each team member simply clears away whatever is on the surface designated for that day, and sorts those items into the "magic" white boxes, grouping the items and labeling the boxes with predetermined categories. We call these boxes "magic" because they are tailor-made for the job of clearing and organizing the house. They are white and neat-looking and tend to blend in with the background of the rooms they are in. They are uniform and are easily stacked. And they are not so big they become too heavy to manage. In short, they are irreplaceable in the organizing process.

The team member writes the category in bold on the outside of each box sitting open on the floor during the work. If because of personal preference you hesitate to write on the surface of the box, you may write on a piece of paper that's been attached to the outside.

Whichever way you prefer to label the boxes, categories may include Shoes, Toys, Clothes, Books, Papers, etc. A trash bag should be placed nearby for obvious debris, such as used paper napkins, broken glass, empty envelopes, expired coupons, and the like. But it's important to also have a box labeled "Trash," where team members can put things that they *think* should be thrown away, but it's not obvious garbage (like a candy wrapper). That way, you still have the opportunity to go through and determine if it's really trash or something more important. You still have the control.

Once a team member clears her designated surface for the day, she is finished. She'll put the tops on the boxes, stack them out of the way, and pat herself on the back for finishing the day's task.

If she has the time, she may begin to work on the next day's surfaces, based on the rules you've outlined for your team. Or she could start helping other team members in their zones.

You'll probably hear team members singing out from room to room, "I'm on Tuesday already!" or "My Monday has hit a problem here. Does anybody have time to help?" Keep it flexible, and you and your team members will have a lot of fun.

Professional Team Members

Most people will choose to enlist friends and/or family members for their team. But some may prefer to call in hired help like a professional organizer. An experienced organizer, who is willing to take over and work within your team guidelines, can be a great asset. Just be sure to make your team approach clear to him or her. If the professional you're considering seems skeptical or reluctant to use the five-day team approach, move on quickly. You can locate a professional organizer in your area by logging on to NAPO.net, the website for National Association of Professional Organizers.

Prices for services vary widely, according to region and experience.

Meanwhile, your team members undoubtedly will have some organizing strengths to bring to the project as they do their primary job—sorting.

Many of us struggle with clutter because we find it difficult to make sorting decisions. It's likely that your team members can bridge that gap for you. Decisions about sorting may come pretty naturally for them, so they'll be able to zip right along. Besides, they won't be emotionally attached to the items, as you are.

Their strengths can be life-changing for you if you harness them properly. Trying to do it alone hasn't worked for you. Many support-group participants who are working on change often remind each other that the definition of insanity is continuing to do the same thing and expecting a different result. We know it's difficult to visualize the power of a group effort in transforming your house. It's just one of those things you have to experience to really understand. This team idea will tip the scale that has, so far, refused to move very far in the right direction for you. But take heart: Using this method can make your goals reality. Really!

On the other hand, as we have said earlier, don't abandon this project if you can't seem to find others to help you. We suggest working alone only when the team approach is absolutely impossible. But if that's your only option, you can still be very successful using the unique body-schema technique presented in the day-to-day schedule. You'll lose the energy and synergy of a group effort, but the organized home of your dreams finally will be within reach!

Details of Day-to-Day Team Tasks

Now it's time to get down to business about the details of this plan. Along with the strategy for each day, you'll also find a related thought that may be helpful for you or your team.

It's important to remember that permanent change comes from the inside, out. Without addressing our inner thoughts and feelings, we either avoid change altogether, or quickly abandon new ways of behavior. The thoughts we've included show more insight into some of the concepts involved in making positive, lasting change. By considering and internalizing them on the days you are working the Mount Rushmore plan, you will be encouraged—and likely, more successful in the long run.

Monday

Today is the day you and your team will start to clear the surfaces in your home that are located in the space found from the feet to the knees. This means: the floor, which is the largest surface in the house; low bookshelves; low tables; footstools; and anything else in your home that's in the area below the knees. Keep in mind that you won't go into cabinets yet. This is the day when you'll simply attack piles on the floor—shoes out of place, children's toys, and containers on the floor that should be in another room.

> **SINCERE PRAYER FOR WHEN THE GOING GETS TOUGH**
>
> *Lord, just for today, help me to put one foot in front of the other and keep going in the right direction a little at a time.*

Armed with instructions and white boxes, position your team members in each room. When instructed to begin, team members will start taking things that do not belong on the floor and low surfaces, and sorting them into the boxes, which they'll label as categories of items become apparent.

Martin's View

As team member Martin set to work on his Monday task, he looked around and began to assess the items in the feet-to-knees region he was supposed to clear. His eyes skimmed over shoes, papers, children's toys, and just plain trash all mixed up and lying on the low surfaces. The bookshelf, especially, was a potpourri of papers. Martin was happy to be sorting things and helping to solve the problem.

He labeled his six boxes based on where they would eventually go. He labeled one "Papers and Magazines," indicating in the lower left that it had come from the living room bookshelf, and labeling in the lower right the room where it would go (a designated office).

He labeled other boxes in the same way, designating categories such as "Children's Shoes," "Toys" (headed ultimately to the play area), "Dog" (to be taken to the place where dog food and accessories were stored), "Trash," and "Question." Later, he had to ask for a couple more boxes, as new categories emerged.

It's important to remember that the box labeled "Trash" is by no means the final word that those items are headed out the door for the garbage. This is the box for things your team member thinks might be trash. Of course, you, as the owner, have the final word. Only the owner can put things from the boxes labeled "Trash" into trash bags intended for a garbage can outside.

Martin's box labeled "Question" was for things that had no obvious place. They would need to be dealt with later, after the rest of the things he was sorting were in their correct locations.

By the end of two hours, Martin had sorted everything in his zone. He cleared shelves, floor surfaces, footstools, and the two lowest bookshelves. He neatly put the lids on the boxes and smiled. He had used his day to help a neighbor, and he was happy with himself.

Thoughts to Move You Forward on Monday

Change is hard. It makes us uncomfortable. What you are undertaking is definitely a change. Shakespeare's *Hamlet* notes that we would "rather bear those ills we have, than fly to others that we know not of." The bard hit a home run on that one!

> "Life is not lost by dying; life is lost minute by minute, day by dragging day, in all the thousand small uncaring ways."
> —Stephen Vincent Benet, American Poet

We live with clutter, and continue habits that encourage it, because it is so hard to take the first step toward another way of life. In order to tolerate the condition of the house, we try to remain comfortable with the visual insults clutter brings. We dull our visual alertness so we won't notice it. We tell ourselves that we don't mind if we can't have people over comfortably, or at all. And endlessly looking for things that are misplaced . . . we learn to tolerate that, as well.

We resist facing the reality—that living with clutter and disorganization is really pretty miserable. Still, we would rather live with it than try to make a change. Especially if we don't know how to make that change and get it to stick.

But now you are through tolerating it. You are willing to consider changing. Your courage is up. Your enthusiasm is beginning to bubble. Keep going!

Maybe you've tried before and run out of steam for one reason or another. You've never finished. Or you finished and your home drifted back into disarray. Or you were sabotaged by others, or by circumstances.

Fear not! This is a surefire plan for success. Let's get going on Monday's job.

Tuesday

Today is the day we hit the big time by clearing all the main surfaces located from the knees to the shoulders. Today, our team will tackle all of the tables, beds, bookcases, bathroom vanities, toilet tops, and windowsills. You get the idea.

Seems like a big job? Don't worry. When the plan comes together, you'll see it works. Imagine it!

You are ready and willing. Now you will be able.

Bernice was selected to be on her godmother's organizing team, headed by a professional organizer.

"It was a fun idea to see if we could get my godmother's home neat in just one week," she recalls. "It seemed like an impossible dream!"

She had not been there on Monday. So when Bernice walked into her godmother's home early on Tuesday, she instantly liked what she saw. There were boxes neatly stacked in each room, labeled to show they held items that previously had been strewn all over the floors. The house already looked neater and felt much lighter.

"Today, you will only sort items that are in the range from your knees to your shoulders," the organizer explained.

It seemed like a strange concept. But with the success she saw from yesterday's work, and feeding on the enthusiasm of the other team members, Bernice was eager to go along with the plan.

"Don't move any items that are above your shoulders, and don't open any cabinets or drawers," the organizer continued. "Also, be sure *not* to throw away anything."

That, Bernice learned, would be the job of "the boss": her godmother.

The way to move forward is to take the next step.

"She'll make all the decisions about throwing away," the organizer affirmed.

Bernice and the rest of the team members set right to work. It was fun, like a contest to see who could sort and box things the fastest. Greg from the next room filled his box labeled "Papers" quickly, then labeled a new box to sit atop the first. Candy quickly sorted and boxed knickknacks that had been sitting on the piano collecting dust. Fabio hummed as he cleared the toys and scattered puzzle pieces from the coffee table in the living room. It was a fun, exciting afternoon, all in the spirit of helping.

"How do I get a team to come to my house?" team member Pamela asked laughingly. "I think everyone needs a team like us!"

The two hours of sorting passed quickly for Bernice and the rest of the team. Everyone had fun. And most important, her godmother's house looked so much neater! Every surface (up to the shoulders) was neatly sorted into the boxes, and her godmother was thrilled!

Bernice wondered out loud, "What is she going to do with all the boxes?"

The organizer smiled and explained that her godmother would have to go through them eventually. But for now, she could have a neat, clutter-free space.

"The next step—the putting away—is much easier when everything is sorted and labeled. It's somehow not so overwhelming," the professional explained.

Bernice's godmother was grateful. All the team members left refreshed and exhilarated, thinking about how much fun they'd had doing something so worthwhile.

Thoughts to Move You Forward on Tuesday

In the process of moving from cluttered chaos to organized calm, discomfort is a natural component. A feeling of uneasiness haunts us as we contemplate beginning. It challenges us while we are in the process. Taking that first step toward a wonderful new way of life is daunting. But why?

As we consider starting to move forward, our desire for progress is challenged by "what ifs":

"If the house is nice, I can have people in. But that can be scary. What if nobody comes if I invite them? Or what if I'm not a talented hostess?"

"I don't want to fail again. What if I can't maintain order after all of these people help me to get it in shape?"

"Will my family cooperate? What if they don't want to change?"

She Faced Her Fear and Did It Anyway

Fear was Elizabeth's issue—she was both afraid to start and afraid not to start. "I'm so embarrassed," she lamented. "I don't want anybody to come into my mess."

Elizabeth's main concern was that people would look down on her. Or worse. They might even ridicule her. She thought that, silently, people would be questioning the same things she'd asked herself about her belongings: You're saving that?! Why? Don't you know it's junk? How stupid you must be to hold on to all of those useless things.

But finally she rallied her courage to invite a team of friends over for a total transformation of her home. And almost instantly she was amazed.

"They made me feel very comfortable," she recalled later. "They made me feel like they just wanted to help me."

After several hours of work, Elizabeth was pleased. Her floors were starting to be clear, and things were being moved into the areas where they ultimately belonged. Surfaces were being cleared, and her house was shaping up nicely.

Looking around her home, Elizabeth admitted, "I'm so happy I let my guard down and allowed help to come in. I've been trying to get rid of that large pile in the mudroom forever! The children come in with toys, and they just end up in a pile. The pile got pushed into the corner and has been growing there for years, but my team got rid of it in a day! I'm so happy!"

Elizabeth risked embarrassment, and ended up a winner. You can, too!

In her book *Feel the Fear and Do It Anyway*, Susan Jeffers encourages this idea of expanding your comfort zone: "Take a risk a day—one small or bold stroke that will make you feel great once you have done it. Even if it doesn't work out the way you wanted it to, at least you've tried. You didn't sit back . . . powerless."[1]

Working the five-day game plan that we propose takes courage. It may be painful at first. But living the way you are now is painful. A messy house brings with it frustration, stress, isolation, confusion, and discouragement.

When your five-day game plan is over and the project is complete, the discomfort you have overcome to get your house organized will open a new world of comfort, beauty, efficiency, the ability to entertain, and a general feeling that your life is now under control. Until your house comes out of the state of confusion it's in now, you won't be able to even imagine the sense of self and the emotional health you'll be able to attain.

Celeste Is a Believer Now

Celeste, a teacher, spent all of her free time working on her clutter. It seemed she never used her time off to do anything she wanted to do. She "cleaned" because she felt the burden of trying to control her house. Battle worn, she finally gave in and let her family help.

Using the team approach, they boxed and sorted for two days, and left Celeste with a comforting, clutter-free home. She had struggled for years and never gotten close to that.

"In only two days, my house went from being a disaster house to being a home I can be proud of!" she rejoiced.

Now Celeste is a believer. Her advice? "Don't be scared! Get up the nerve to let the people who love you, help you!"

She also admonishes us to "up the pride." Well said, Celeste.

Expect some turbulence on your journey. Be willing to travel a twisting road of emotions on the way to a wonderful new way of life.

It helps to know that mistakes might be made. This is not unusual. You may change your mind about a discarded item, or may feel something has been misplaced. You may feel uncomfortable. At least, these things may happen if you're doing it boldly. If you're a perfectionist to the core, you must be willing to live with those possibilities—and continue moving forward.

Expect discouragements at certain parts of your adventure. You may get tired or want to stop while your crew is still gung ho. You may want to micromanage. But those, or other minor problems, don't have to trip you up.

If you are going after this task with enthusiasm, some failure and mistakes are a good sign! In fact, if you don't make mistakes in certain parts of the process, that's a sign that you're being far too cautious. Too much caution may cause you to get cold feet and stop the process.

During the five-day process, you'll probably feel you've run aground—not just once, but several times. Any big project has its ups and downs. That is to be expected. Maybe you will start to feel nervous about the entire project. Maybe you will feel you are losing focus. Maybe you have a disagreement with one of the team members; one of the team members doesn't come back; or a room is left a little messy during the process. Any one of these things, or others, can cause you to feel uncomfortable. Don't give up hope . . . stay the course . . . have faith in the process. Remember that fear can be an acronym for False Evidence Appearing Real.

Don't let any of these things stop you. It is said that only two kinds of sailors never run aground. One kind never left port. The others were liars. Expect problems, but keep going!

Wednesday

On Wednesday your team will clear all surfaces between the shoulders and the ceiling—but without opening any cabinets or drawers. The goal is to look up . . . to the higher surfaces in your home.

This day's task is to sort and move all things that don't belong on the refrigerator top, the tops of bookcases, shelves in the laundry room, upper closet racks, or any other surfaces that are high—from your shoulders up.

You may think this doesn't include much surface area, but look around. You just might be amazed.

Teens Jared and Sophia came together to work with their team for the first time on Wednesday. It was part of their community service requirement for high school graduation to help Mrs. Crowley, an elderly lady on the first floor of their high-rise condo.

When they entered the house, they saw the result of the previous days' work: clear, neat surfaces with boxes stacked against every wall. But when they looked up to the higher surfaces, they saw clutter, clutter, clutter! The surfaces were dusty and full of stuff!

Armed with determination and a willing spirit, they joined in the "huddle" to get their instructions for Wednesday and be brought up to speed on the ground rules for volunteers.

Mrs. Crowley seemed confident and eager to get everyone on board. She had been through two days of having helpers and now knew the game plan. She explained that on Monday morning she had no faith that her cluttered home really could be made pleasant and neat. But by Monday afternoon, she began to have hope. On Tuesday, she was amazed. And now, on Wednesday, she was not only confident, but she inspired confidence in all the volunteers.

"When you get started, sort only the surfaces that are from your shoulders to the ceiling," she explained. "Today we are looking up! And I'm looking forward to it!"

Sofia was assigned to the office and Jared to the kitchen, because of his height. He would be able to reach the shelving that went around the perimeter.

"You can just throw out all of the plastic fruit and flowers," Mrs. Crowley said with a happy twinkle in her eyes, pointing to several high shelves piled with dusty plastic fruit and fading plastic flowers. She was relieved to see them go.

Her enthusiasm was contagious, and soon everyone was sorting energetically. Boxes were quickly filled and labeled, so she could make decisions about their contents later. As Sofia, Jared, and the other team members were busy grouping items into boxes, Mrs. Crowley was going through the boxes labeled "Trash." She threw almost everything from those into the large black garbage bags. But every now and then, the volunteers would hear her say, "Ah, I was looking for that!" or, "That's a piece to . . ."

After two hours of sorting papers from the top of the credenza and the top of the bookshelves, Sofia was tired and ready to go home for a rest. Jared, on the other hand, was energized, excited, and not ready to stop.

Whether tired or excited, everyone left feeling really good about the help they'd provided. And Mrs. Crowley was ecstatic. She had a new lease on life, and vowed to go through each box and make the decisions necessary to get rid of the clutter. She didn't want to leave a burden of clutter for her children to deal with later.

Jared volunteered to help Mrs. Crowley one day a week, as she sorted through labeled boxes. He kept his promise. And after two months of going box by box, Mrs. Crowley's home was neatly organized, and Jared felt like a million dollars!

> "You see, but you do not observe."
> —Sherlock Holmes to Dr. Watson, "Scandal in Bohemia" by Sir Arthur Conan Doyle

Thoughts to Move You Forward on Wednesday

Six Steps to an Organized Life

RE-CRYSTALLIZE YOUR DESIRE

Ask yourself that all-important question again: "If everything were perfect and my house was exactly the way I want it, what would it look like?" Pull together your specific wants for your house by going from room to room and visualizing the change. Say it aloud. Find and post magazine pictures that represent how you want your house to look. You might even write it out and create a project book to store the ideas.

REEVALUATE WHERE YOU ARE NOW

Write a list of problems that still remain in each room. Or take a picture of how the room looks now. Maybe do both. Post them somewhere in the room or in your house project book.

Psychologists have found that people can overlook clutter when they're simply looking at their surroundings, but they can see it clearly in photos.

Sara Jo stumbled upon the power of taking pictures. She shared her discovery with members of an online support group for people who battle messiness but desperately want to be organized:

Just wanted to share with y'all: Something I did kind of "frightened" me into finally getting going.

I (still) believe I'm just a messy clutterer. However, I took some photos of my messy house, and when I did—uh-oh! The photos look just like all those homes on *Hoarders* and *Oprah* and the other shows about messy homes.

No, I am *not* totally buried. I can still walk through my home. But it's time to clean it out now, before it gets worse. And that's what I'm doing.

So if you look at one of those shows and think, *I'm not that bad,* take your digital camera and snap a few photos. Wait a couple days and look at those photos on your computer. (You can delete 'em fast.) Then decide if it's time to do something, either on your own or with some help.

Sara Jo was right. Pictures can sound a mighty wake-up call.

RE-COMMIT TO A FIRM DECISION

Don't skip this step. Verbalize or write out what you are willing to do in order to change the condition of your house. Are you maintaining your desire to apply the steps of this program as they fit into your situation?

Finish this question, numbering your list of promises: "In order to change the condition of my house, I will . . ." Put your written response in your project book.

RE-DEFINE AND CHALLENGE YOUR HINDRANCES

Fears, circumstances, and personal characteristics have caused you to make decisions that have led to clutter. List those specifically.

- My fears

  _____

- My circumstances

  _____

- My personal characteristics

  _____

Go down your list of hindrances. State or write your mental challenges and how you can make physical changes for each problem so the challenges will lose power over your life.

MAKE IT HAPPEN

The things that turn a wish into a path toward change are having a time line and implementing an action plan. List action steps you plan to take and when you aim to accomplish each step, even if the deadline is tentative. Add that to your project book.

Begin working your plan, step by step.

GET HELP

Enlisting the help of a team, whether large or small, is an integral part of the Mount Rushmore program. However, you may want to start by asking a trusted friend to help you crystallize your dreams now, and encourage you to keep on track as you work the steps of this program. A professional counselor or coach could also advise you as you go along.

Thursday

We're almost through the week! It's time to get busy sorting and clearing the interior surfaces of your home. You should be breathing a sigh of relief because, by now, all of the visible surfaces of your home should be cleared and things should be looking much better.

Today we'll open cabinets, drawers, cupboards, etc. We'll look inside closets. We'll tackle closet shelves and vanity drawers. At this point the house has made a U-turn, and we're able to think about more than order. We can start to think about beauty and entertaining and other happy thoughts of the future.

Claudia's Thursday Experience

Upon entering Claudia's tiny apartment, Yolanda wondered why she had been invited to join the "Team to Clean." Claudia's home was very neat, with boxes lined up along every wall. Some boxes said "From the Kitchen"; some said "From the Bathroom"; some said "From the Bedroom." Other than the boxes, the surfaces were clean and the apartment was airy.

But after receiving instructions for the day, Yolanda understood. At first glance, the apartment only appeared clutter-free. But the internal areas still needed attention. Today was the day to box and sort interior surfaces. And boy did they need it!

Before the crew arrived, Claudia had slapped a sticky note on the front of each cabinet and drawer noting what belonged there. The team member now knew what kinds of things should stay, and could easily recognize what was out of place.

Yolanda's station was the bathroom. When she opened the under-sink cabinet, she saw it was filled to the brim. There were bottles of all sizes, filled with everyday toiletries, lotions, and medicinal ointments. Many of the bottles were duplicates. And there were cleaning products galore. What was she supposed to do? Consolidate? Discard?

She remembered her instructions: "Don't throw anything away—Claudia will do that. Don't make decisions for her. Instead, ask."

Yolanda asked, and Claudia gave her permission to consolidate when possible, and put partially used items in a box labeled "Maybe." Happy with that, Yolanda began sorting and consolidating. The box labeled "Trash" was used to hold the things Yolanda thought should be thrown away. Claudia went through those to make final decisions. Sometimes she agreed, sometimes she decided to keep things. Claudia left one of each of the necessary toiletries where they belonged.

Sometimes it was tempting for Yolanda to say, "You should throw that away. It's junk," or "It's no good anymore," or "There's not enough to keep." But she understood that for this plan to be effective, she was not allowed to judge. It was not her job to make decisions for Claudia; her job was to help Claudia quickly clear the interior surfaces of her home.

While Yolanda was sorting the bathroom items, there were others sorting in the kitchen, office, and small master bedroom. By the end of the day, all cabinets, drawers, and interior surfaces in Claudia's home were cleared out, and more boxes were placed along the walls.

As Yolanda and the other volunteers were leaving, Claudia gave each of them a parting thank-you gift. She was so grateful for what they'd given her—the gift of nonjudgmental assistance.

Thoughts to Move You Forward on Thursday

Toss the Free Spirit and Grab Proven Pathways

Learning and following organizing rules is more important than people think, because natural abilities aren't enough for most of us.

People in general, and especially disorganized people, have more confidence in their ability to function successfully than they ought to have. We disorganized types especially enjoy living as free spirits, flying by the seat of our pants, kicking over the traces, whatever figure of speech you want to use to describe how we don't like to function in regimented ways. And that can be a charming part of our exuberant personalities.

But in the organizational realm, this does not work well, if at all. Like it or not, it's time we wake up to that fact and hitch our organizational wagons to horses that lead us down a proven systematic path of success.

In their intriguing book *The Invisible Gorilla*, research psychologists Christopher Chabris and Daniel Simons show that we often go astray when we count on our senses to help us function. Because many disorganized people are quite intelligent (the personal opinion of the authors—not proven scientifically, as yet) and tend to be free spirits, they think they can wing the organizing process without changing their behavior with "annoying and constraining" organizing techniques. They could not be more wrong.

Here's the truth about places where we need to be cautious in the organizing process.

USING YOUR MEMORY

People in general tend to rely too much on memory to find what they need. This was true with Leah. Leah constantly said to herself, "I'll remember where I put this, so I don't need to bother to put it in a predetermined place." She often reasoned, "I don't have a special place for it, so I'll leave it here because it's more convenient. I'll need it in a minute, anyway."

Because she didn't have a designated place she used consistently, she chose places for things on the fly. Frequently she forgot where she put something because she never actually focused on where she was placing it when she set it down. Then she would end up saying things like, "Where is my wallet? I just had it! How can things disappear like that?"

Like Leah, if we don't create places for our things, our minds will move on to other things during the nanosecond we took to put an item "right here for just a second." Later, we have trouble remembering which "special place" we used last for that item, because we never really noticed where we put it.

The only cure is the tried-and-true method that is the backbone of this program—grouping like things together. The screwdriver can be easily misplaced when left outside "for just a minute" where the last project was done. But if Leah, and free spirits like her, could thoroughly convince themselves that it's worthwhile to take the time to put that screwdriver back in a container labeled "Building Tools," their lives would be transformed.

There are two basic kinds of memory: short term and long term. Short-term memory is very fluid and lasts only thirty seconds or a little more. It can only store about five to nine items at a time. Anything that needs to be recalled at a later time must go to one of the many long-term memory storehouses around the brain, depending on the kind of memory it is—visual, auditory, sequential, etc.

You can transform short-term memory (like a person's name) into long-term memory by repeating it (maybe several times), or thinking of an association or trick (such as picturing your new neighbor, Carol, with a Christmas wreath around her head). There are many resources that describe how to use mnemonic devices to boost your memory skills.

But what about remembering things stored in the house? It's one of the most important skills of living an organized life. . . .

"Where did I put that important paper?"

"Have you seen the scissors?"

"Anybody know where my keys are?"

"Has somebody moved my purse?"

"How can things just disappear?!"

For remembering the location of various items around the house, the very best memory approach is the device known by experts as *chunking*. Chunking simply means grouping things that are alike in one chunk, so you don't have to remember where each item is. You simply need to remember where "things like that" are kept. For instance, all sewing supplies are grouped in one area, all papers in another, all cleaning supplies in yet another. The more chunking you use in setting up your home, the more organized and usable your house will be.

The "magic" white boxes get their power from chunking. You'll see this powerful approach applied more and more as we follow the plan to bring your house under control. So if you're not going to chuck something, chunk it—so you can recall what you've done with it.

Visual Alertness

Does the saying "If it were a snake it would have bitten me" mean anything to you? It means it's there, but you overlook it. We *look*, but we don't see or notice.

The reason we don't notice things has to do with how we focus our attention. It's what researchers Chabris and Simons call "unintentional blindness." The point is: Don't leave something sitting out as an aid to being able to locate it later. Instead, place it with similar items.

Overconfidence in Our Abilities

Being typically upbeat and capable people, we place more confidence in our ability to handle our clutter problem than we should. We tell ourselves that we will get the place in order just as soon as we get around to it . . . when we get enough time, energy, or desire.

Or we feel that we can manage to live a satisfactory life, even in the midst of the disorganized clutter that's still accumulating. We try to convince ourselves that we can live a normal life in abnormal surroundings. But an I-can-do-it attitude is misplaced when it's used to sidestep a chronic problem, such as the clutter we face every day.

A common word found in the vocabulary of those who finally face the issue of their clutter is *overwhelmed*. In Messies Anonymous, those who follow the twelve steps that have been adapted with permission from Alcoholics Anonymous start with Step One, which states the recognition that "we are powerless over clutter and disorganization in our lives, and that our lives have become unmanageable." We have tried every approach we know, and yet we still struggle with clutter. Once admitting "The way I'm doing this just isn't working," we are on the road to recovery, or, twelve-step users say, we're being "restored to sanity."

As long as we're sure we can do it our way if we just try harder, we're doomed to continue the same unsuccessful struggle with clutter. We have to step out of the condition some call "unskilled and unaware." We have to become fully aware of the condition of the house and our inability to keep it under control. Then we are ready to step into success. Because we are capable, and maybe even gifted in many areas of life, our difficulty in this one area of housekeeping is hard to comprehend, and the knowledge that we are powerless in this area takes a long time to accept.

Once we face our situation honestly, we have already begun to change because we are now thinking differently. Sanity has started to creep into our lives. Once that happens, we are ready to abandon the old familiar ways and follow a proven system, like the one outlined in this book.

Friday

Today is the last day! The final hurrah in our five-days-to-a-clean-house program!

If you've followed the plan, your surfaces are uncluttered. You can open your drawers and cabinets and actually find things. Everything is finally neat! You can have guests over, even have a party . . . things you've longed to do! And getting there wasn't so painful.

But in most houses, there is one more area of concern. On our final day, we'll go beyond the working areas of the house to the storage areas. We'll focus on the surfaces in the attic, utility room, and garage. Once again, we'll sort, consolidate, and put things where they belong. We'll take the wrong things away and replace them with the right things—things that actually belong in that space.

Remember that today the goal is to box things, label the boxes, and make things neat. We will not be able to organize a cluttered garage or storage unit in an afternoon, but we can consolidate and make the areas neat.

Mr. Norman's Garage Adventure

Roland came prepared. Gloves and dust mask in hand, he looked forward to helping his long-time neighbor, Mr. Norman, get his garage in shape. Over the years, Mr. Norman would make jokes about his garage. But the jokes had lost their humor, and Mr. Norman was getting up in years. Roland had always wanted to help him but didn't know how to offer, without possibly having the offer sound offensive. So Roland said nothing.

But when his Sunday school class took on Mr. Norman's garage as their annual project, Roland was thrilled. And today was the day!

At the beginning of the day, the team leader started with the instructions: "Don't throw anything away. Mr. Norman will make those decisions. You just sort items into boxes." Roland was, at first, certain that the plan wouldn't make a big difference. After all, he thought, the only way to clean up a massively cluttered garage was to throw things away. But what he discovered was very interesting. By sorting and boxing, Mr. Norman could see what he had in a neutral, almost peaceful way. Soon, instead of resisting others telling him to throw his things away, he started saying, "I really don't need this! What did I ever see in this? Why keep something that doesn't work? Why do I need three of these?" By asking himself those questions, Mr. Norman could more easily discard his things without anyone putting pressure on him.

The team was instructed not to sift through what was already in boxes. Mr. Norman's plan was to go through all of the boxes at the same time. The newly sorted boxes were properly labeled and placed along a vacant wall, until every-thing left in the garage was boxed up neatly.

Now Mr. Norman's garage was no longer an eyesore to the community every time he opened it, and Mr. Norman was a happy, grateful neighbor.

Use a team to tackle your garage or any other storage unit like a shed, attic, utility room, or even an off-site storage unit.

Thoughts to Move You Forward on Friday

Identify Your Clutter Spots and Eliminate Them

Clutter is not just a generic term. There are different types. If you analyze the different types of clutter and pinpoint the ones that affect you most, you will be further down the line in solving your problems. Nobody gets very far when rambling around in a fog mumbling, "Something's got to be done about this." Let's look at three types of clutter and what can be done about each.

SITUATION-BASED CLUTTER

Some situations can impose disorganization on even the most organized people. These situations can overwhelm any-body and cry out, especially, for a team approach.

The situation may be kids coming home from college, an adult child moving back in with his or her belongings, an adult parent moving. It may be the aftermath of a flood or devastating storm. Anything that comes into life that our houses cannot easily absorb can create clutter.

Melody experienced a situational crash in her life, as four generations of her family came to live in her 1,700-square-foot house. It started when Melody's parents moved in. About the same time, Melody's daughter got a divorce and moved back home with her newborn. Both groups dumped their belongings in the basement in the hurry of their changes.

Melody's approach was to pick up a few things she could place upstairs each time she came up from the basement. But it wasn't enough. Very, very little progress was being made in clearing the basement.

This situation called for a focused family day, in order to apply a variation of the basic Mount Rushmore program to their specific situation. Again, the key was to bring some order to the clutter, and clear all surfaces by grouping the items into those magic white boxes.

For two days Melody's family worked, separating items by owner and grouping like items together, labeling and stacking each box.

Once everything was boxed and the boxes were stacked against the wall, the family team met in the storage area to work on de-junking and unloading the white boxes. The items that needed to go to rooms in the main area of the house were removed from the boxes, and the ones that needed to stay stored were grouped in their places, according to who the owner was.

The entire process took a week . . . but what a difference it made! After it was over, everyone was happier and more comfortable. "It helped that we were all doing it together. It made it feel like it was less work, and added an element of fun to an otherwise tedious project. And we are all happy that it is over!"

For cleaning up situational disorganization, follow this step-by-step action plan:

1. Get a "clean perspective" by boxing everything. Stick on a general label as you go, with notes like "Ginny's Stuff," "Roberto's Things," "Dad's Personal Items," "Foodstuffs," etc. If it's really bad, don't get too particular with your labeling. The point is to make clear which spaces need more work and to get an emotional breath of fresh air, bringing some sanity to the mayhem.

2. Make a plan about what you're going to do with the things in the boxes. Designate a specific time each day or week to get together. Each person on the team should handle one box in each visit to the work area. Boxes of paper generally take about an hour per box. Handle boxes of paper last.

3. Unbox according to the plan, taking the needed things out and re-boxing the items according to specific ownership, so each person feels that he or she can access their items if necessary. Store the boxes according to owner.

Emotionally Based Clutter

Often messes arise when we keep items—more than we can handle—that connect us emotionally in some way to important people in our lives.

Sometimes those remembered relationships are warm and fuzzy, as in Sam's case. He saved everything that related to his children, now grown, in an attempt to keep alive his memories of when they were together as a family.

Bertha kept gifts received from a loved one, drawings, gifts from children, cards and letters, even belongings someone else left behind after death. To her, the belongings were part of those relationships.

The items we retain keep the memory of our loved ones fresh and remind us of their place in our lives. The items have deep roots in our hearts. But they sit around our houses cluttering the surfaces, and sometimes making us miserable.

Sometimes the items are part of a complex and disappointing relationship, or represent opportunities that have not been resolved. Wayward children, lost love ones, a time in our lives when things were better. Until we are able to make peace with those issues, we hold on to the items from the place we got "stuck." In these cases, it's almost impossible to voluntarily let go, to get unstuck.

Rhonda was unable to let go of her deceased father's clothes that were crowding her small apartment closet. Every time she handled his belongings, memories flooded back. Some were good memories, and she longed to reminisce with him again. Others were not so pleasant, and she wished she could hug him and put those bad feelings behind her. To let his things go was admitting that none of that would be possible now.

Our best solution in these cases is to avoid altogether the problem of trying to let go. Instead—you guessed it—we can box those items in our magic white boxes and label the contents. Most people who want clear surfaces are willing to store items, as long as they don't have to make a final parting with the memory icons. Over time, the physical items that carry a memory often release their hold on us because they have been out of sight and we have moved on. It's then that we're able to appropriately let go.

"But," you may say, "where can I put these boxes? There's no room!" The truth is, there's always room. But you might have to move or condense some of the other things you're already storing. Look in other boxes, bags, or drawers and see if you have unused space. You may have to turn existing boxes sideways to make room for another box. If you expect this to be difficult for you, keep in mind that you are already storing these items, just in a messy, disheveled way. With the box system, you're simply storing them in a better,

> There ain't no organizer fairy who can stuff more than will physically fit into your house.

more accessible way that honors the relationship more than the messy, dusty, dishonoring way. Storing neatly is better than storing messy.

PHYSICAL (ENVIRONMENTAL) CLUTTER

Sometimes the source of clutter is the result of the physical attributes of your home. Perhaps you have a house that is too small for the number of people living there and the belongings you all have. Maybe it's so large that it invites you to collect more than you should. Or maybe your house has virtually no closets or is in disrepair. Sometimes an environmental issue is something as simple as not addressing the problem of enough drawer or closet space. As you fill up space with furniture to make your house your home, keep in mind that you need drawers, cubbies, cabinets, and shelves to keep belongings neatly organized.

A note of caution is necessary when we talk about furniture. Sometimes having too much furniture just adds to the clutter. Having too many chairs, dressers, and plastic containers becomes part of the problem. Finding the right balance between having enough of the right kind of furniture for storage and having too much furniture requires perspective. Look at the houses of friends whose homes you admire. Check out magazine pictures. Ask for opinions of trusted friends. As the house clears up, so will your perspective on this issue.

Maybe you were able to keep the house organized until the baby arrived. Maybe it was baby number two or three who threw you off organizationally. In many families, the house becomes too small over time for the number of people or belongings. Chaos ensues.

Because disorganized people tend to be the cerebral sort, we often disregard the importance of the physical environment in which we function. Evaluate whether you are trying to organize in a situation that no organizationally savvy person would even attempt. Too much furniture? Subtract it. Too little storage? Add it. Hard to access what you need? Change it. Do whatever it takes to get the job done.

The most important approach is to realize that changes need to be made in your thinking and behavior. Even though it can be difficult to face, reality dictates that you have no choice but to pare down how many items you keep, and rev up your diligence about keeping surfaces clear. There ain't no organizer fairy who can stuff more than will physically fit into your house.

Jen finally saw this, realizing she had two beneficial qualities that had boomeranged to her disadvantage. She was creative . . . and frugal. When she needed storage containers, she created them with plastic, wood, or cardboard pieces she had grouped in piles sitting around the house. When she opened her eyes to the fact that her successfully organized friends did not indulge in this kind of storage creativity, she realized that she was sidestepping the importance of a commitment to adequate storage. No more coffee-can planters, bean-can pencil holders, empty plastic hummus containers to hold change.

When she broke through her rigid frugality and began to purchase storage designed for the purpose of home organizing, her eyes were opened to a whole new way of efficient living.

Take a look at what your organized friends use to stay organized, then go and do likewise.

Saturday

Welcome to the clutter-free side of the world! Now you can actually glimpse in your own home how the other half lives. You never thought you would be here, especially not this fast. Congratulations to you!

Now . . . it's time to celebrate!

Here are some things to do:

1. Take a deep breath. Appreciate your courage and the stamina it took for you to finally do it. You are amazing!
2. Start the process of building on your new foundation of order. To help you maintain order, it is essential that you add a routine for cleanliness. A unique cleaning schedule kit called the Super Flipper is available through messies.com. How is this unique? You start creating a cleaning routing by listing just three jobs a day that should be done. Just doing those, along with three regular—such as making the bed, doing the dishes, and washing the laundry—will make a remarkable change.

We'll discuss more on how to be proactive with keeping the house clean and tidy in section 2.

3. Celebrate! Throw a party at your "new" house. You deserve it! Show off all of your hard work before you tackle the next task of emptying the boxes. We define *party* as any deliberate inviting of people into the house for social purposes. You may want to invite a neighbor for a cup of tea or coffee, the team members over for pizza, or friends in for a special occasion. For most disorganized people, being able to have people in without tension about the condition of the house calls for some kind of celebration. Yes!

Consider Juanita's experience. At the end of her Mount Rushmore week, Juanita tearfully sat back and said thank-you to team members again and again. She couldn't believe how far they had come! Her house was beautiful. She could find things. She was oh so proud of herself and the courage it took to allow fellow knitting club members into the house to help her organize.

"They didn't seem to mind at all," she said gratefully. "No one judged me, no one said anything unkind. I spent years imagining that people would ridicule me if they only knew . . . and it didn't happen! All that worry was for nothing!"

Juanita reflected over the happenings of the week. On Monday her house was a disaster, though she had tried to pick up some before the team members arrived. On that first day, the team cleared the surfaces from the floor to the low tables. After the first day, her house seemed to have a little more air.

On Tuesday, the higher surfaces were tackled. And by the end of the day on Tuesday, her house was well on its way to looking good. By Wednesday afternoon, her house was neat; it didn't look like it had ever been cluttered. It was an amazing week!

Just when she thought it couldn't get any better, Thursday came. And by the time her team left, all of her cabinets and drawers were neat, with all of the proper items left in place. She had white boxes full of duplicates, excesses, and broken things to evaluate. She couldn't imagine what she might find in those boxes, but she was sure that with her newfound enthusiasm, when she began to tackle them she would be able to move them out of her house.

> Ironically, our desire to maintain beauty in the small things can end up destroying beauty overall.

Friday was another wonder: The team tackled her outdoor storage unit. At the end of the day, she could walk in and actually find things. What a happy day! What a happy week!

It was time to celebrate, and Juanita was up to the task. She happily began making plans for a party. She made a list of everyone who had helped her transform her home, and she excitedly planned all the food she would prepare—now that she could use her counters and find her mixing bowls. She could be ready to entertain by the very next weekend.

Thoughts to Move You Forward on Saturday

The Power of Beauty in Your Home

We all want order in our lives; we want control over what is frustrating and overwhelming. But practicality is not the only reason. We have an aesthetic reason, as well. We want to be able to express our best selves in our own individual decorating style.

In disgust, a frustrated single woman wrote in an email: "My general problem is that I don't have a decor of any kind . . . just general chaos and clutter. I'm sure I could make the stuff work together, if I could just pull my mind together and organize my junky house."

Somewhere deep inside, once the hope of organization is confirmed, we long for more. We long for beauty.

Beauty is not a yes or no option for the healthy soul. Something within us is invigorated when our eye catches sight of a charming room, a beautifully set table, shining surfaces with balanced decor, or a lovely garden. We're like William Wordsworth, who rhapsodized poetically that at the sight of a field of flowers, his heart was filled with pleasure and it "danced with the daffodils."[2]

Those of us who live surrounded by disorder yet still maintain optimism and vigor . . . well, that says a lot about our natural stamina—and positive outlook! Not everybody can keep going as we do under these conditions.

There is no doubt about it. Clutter is ugly and disheartening, but clear and shining surfaces inspire. The play of dappled shadows on a clean carpet gladdens in a way that is difficult to define or explain intellectually. But the heart confirms it's true when, like Wordsworth's, it dances with pleasure at the sight.

Author and naturalist John Muir has said, "Everybody needs beauty, as well as bread, places to play in and pray in, where nature may heal and give strength to the body and soul."[3]

"We fly to beauty as an asylum from the terrors of finite nature," writes Ralph Waldo Emerson.[4] Healing. Strength. Asylum. What words to cheer the soul!

The irony is that many who are messy and live in clutter often do so because of an intense—but misguided—appreciation of beauty. Because so many items seem lovely—and therefore valuable—we tend to keep more than we can handle neatly. Ironically, our desire to maintain beauty in the small things can end up destroying beauty overall. Often, surfaces that are designed to be free of all but a few select items become covered with many interesting "finds" that, frankly, make it a mess.

Use your own natural sensitivity to beauty to your advantage in doing this five-day project. The trick is to refocus from the nearsighted view of individual items to the overall environment, with the aim of making it supportive of a healthy social and personal life. This is not easy to do.

> Wake up to the beauty you can create. It will transform your organizational life.

That was what Reina discovered. She had difficulty handling complexity. It was much less complicated for her to focus on individual, beautiful objects one at a time than it was for her to notice or even create an overall beautiful environment with clear and well-arranged surfaces.

The team who cleared her home helped bring beauty overall. As areas cleared, she began to see possibilities. She was able to run her ideas by some of the members of the team. Though she was careful not to crowd her clear surfaces, decorating ideas from magazines and television shows now were able to be applied to her house. Once she got her house in a lovely condition and found how nice it was to enjoy neatness, she came to appreciate how a well-ordered house reflects beauty much more than one "beautiful" item.

The longer we keep our houses beautiful and in order, the more we value what it means to us. Your love of that kind of beauty will grow the longer you are surrounded by it. As we get used to it, we begin to value what we have done. Wake up to the beauty you create. It will transform your organizational life. The second section of the book will address the topic of how you can keep your newly neat home beautiful.

Beth Is Ecstatic

Beth H. shared this report after using the five-day team approach to transforming her home:

> The week has come and gone, and my house is now a different home from what it was when we began. My team came in like angels and swooped through every room of the house. They made it livable again. Piles I haven't touched in years melted before my eyes, as they boxed things up in every room. I never felt uncomfortable because I always knew where everything was, and I knew they wouldn't throw my things away.
>
> The thing that amazed me was that they could make everything fit in each room! Clutter that had been everywhere is now neatly in boxes, either lining my hallway or in rooms where their contents belong. I am ecstatic! I can finally use my family room, my storage shed, and my guest bedroom! The rest of the house looks great, too!

By now, the surfaces in your home will be clear. Belongings are grouped and located in the proper rooms. A wonderful victory in the clutter war has been won.

But like Beth, you have boxes to be dealt with. The next chapter addresses what in military parlance is the "mopping up" operation, moving from boxes to real, organized living.

5

What Do I Do Now
With the Stuff in the Boxes?

Your house looks great! But now arises the question that has
been on your mind all along: "What do I do now with all of
these boxes full of stuff?"

This is the defining moment. Look around your house full
of freshly packed boxes, loaded with things sorted this week.
(You may also have some "stale" boxes you stuffed long ago
with excess. We'll deal with those later.)

The "fresh," carefully labeled boxes are stacked neatly
along walls in rooms where their contents ultimately will be
stored. You may have ten boxes or two hundred, depending
on how much clutter you had in your formerly messy home.
The plan now is for you to open each box, one by one, and
empty it.

Before we begin the unpacking process, you need to understand one important tip: Some boxes don't absolutely have to be unpacked. It's possible to live for a very long time using the boxes in the same way you would use a chest of drawers, opening them only when you need something found inside.

As you use the items out of the boxes, put them where they belong permanently. After a while, the things left unused in the boxes have pretty much disqualified themselves as useful—they're obviously useless to you because you haven't needed them. Because they have spent so much time unused, they may have begun to lose their importance in your eyes. That may make it easier to discard those items now.

This is a great way to separate the wheat from the chaff, so to speak. Now you may be willing to pick up a whole box of what has proven to be chaff and take those things to charity to be put to good use in someone else's life. This is a slow but painless way to empty the boxes. It's especially good for those who really struggle with decision making.

Making the Boxes Disappear

You probably don't want to live with boxes stacked against the wall, unpacking them slowly only as you need things. You want them gone so you can put your house totally in order. Good! Encourage yourself to get down to business as soon as possible, and unpack as many of the labeled boxes as quickly as you can. They will melt like snow in the warmth of a spring day. But remember, the contents they're holding did not accumulate overnight . . . and the boxes won't be emptied in one day. It's a day-by-day job. But you are up to the task!

How long will it take? Normally we figure on about an hour per box of papers. It may take less time if your boxes are filled with bulkier things. Use this estimate as a guide in calculating the maximum amount of time it will take you to empty your boxes.

Now you may be asking yourself, "So how do I do it?" Well, for every box being emptied, you will need to have three more of those much-used white boxes in front of you. (You will be using and re-using those boxes again and again!) Label these boxes as follows: "Yes" (I want it), "No" (it's leaving—definitely!), and "Maybe" (I don't know right now if it's staying or leaving).

Here Are the Steps:

Step 1—Set up, open, and label your three empty white boxes: "Yes," "No," and "Maybe." Also, place an empty trash bag nearby.

Step 2—Open the target box you plan to empty. Begin dividing its contents into the labeled boxes.

Into the "Yes" box put everything you want to keep. Most items should already have a place to live in your home. If it doesn't, create a place. Keep the chunking method in mind, grouping like items in the same category.

Into the "Maybe" box put items you're not sure you want. You'd like to delay these decisions until later. This box will also include things that you want but have no specific place for.

Into the "No" box put all the items you don't want and are ready to throw away. This is the right place for things that are duplicates, outdated, useless to you, ugly, dried up, unopened for years, etc. It also includes things that are "good" but not good enough to take up your limited storage space. And this box might hold things that someone else will appreciate . . . just not you. Things that are broken and not fixable should be discarded.

Step 3—When the target box is empty, your task is to empty the "Yes" and "No" boxes immediately. Don't put these boxes out of the way and let them get "cold."

"Yes" box—Put these items in the correct place in your home.

"No" box—Right away, put these items

(a) in the trash,
(b) in the place designated for giveaways,
(c) in the place designated for charity,
(d) set aside for a garage sale or consignment shop, or
(e) in the recycle bin.

Step 4—Focus now on the "Maybe" box. Note on the outside label a few of the items inside.

When this box is full, put the top on it and put it aside. Important: Don't overfill or leave the top off, because you will be stacking these for future review. Use only boxes in good condition for the "Maybe" boxes. Leave them stacked neatly for a pleasant, symmetrical look.

Step 5—Go through all target boxes until you have only "Maybe" boxes remaining. This will probably leave you with about one-third of the total number you had when you started.

Now you've really pared down your collection of boxes. You have much less to deal with, and you can set aside time to start over with the "Maybe" boxes, using the Yes, No, and Maybe method.

The reason this method works is simple: You are delaying the hard decisions. As you go through this process, the items in the "Maybe" box will begin to look different to you. You will have had more practice in decision making, and you'll have seen these items at least once before. Over time, many will begin to lose their appeal, and you will be able to let go of them more easily.

As you go through this process, you naturally begin to evaluate things in a different way. Decisions that once seemed impossible become easier over time. It's a hidden benefit of the process of developing your "organizing muscle."

JEFFREY FACES THE BIG 4-0 WITH A GOAL

As Jeffrey's fortieth birthday approached, he wanted to have a party to celebrate. But first he wanted to clean up the mess in his house.

He knew anticipation of the impending party would keep him motivated. His targeted mess consisted mainly of twelve unsorted and unlabeled storage boxes stacked along the wall of his entertainment room. They had been there as long as he could remember—for sure since he'd moved into the house twelve years before. They contained things he had schlepped with him every time he moved: souvenirs from vacations, college mementos, and more, mostly stuff that didn't belong anywhere, particularly in his house.

He judged it would take about an hour to find places for the things in each box. That was twelve hours of work. He set aside two hours each Saturday for six weeks, and planned to have the party on the seventh Saturday.

Nervous and reluctant, he opened the first box full of papers, badges from former jobs, trinkets, trophies, and a mishmash of other assorted but pretty much useless items. One item at a time, he dropped them into Yes, No, and Maybe boxes he'd set up in front of him.

The next box was a little harder. Letters from his mom and old yearbooks were placed lovingly into a Yes box. He decided he would make a file for the letters from his mother and put his yearbooks on an available bookshelf. After each sorting session, he shuttled the things from the Yes box into their proper places. Letters from long-ago sweethearts and other unimportant things went into the No box and were moved out of the house. He was relieved to find that there was a lot of junk he could toss right into the trash or re-cycle cans.

The work got easier week after week, box after box. He found that he was using the Maybe box less and less as his decision-making ability improved. He ended up with one box of undecideds that he put in the back of his closet to be dealt with another day.

On week number seven, Jeffrey welcomed his guests as he began his forty-first year.

Helpful Tips for Emptying the Boxes

Be realistic. Slowing down and verbalizing your goals can help you make your "I want to keep this" decision more reasonable. Try asking the following questions:

- Why am I keeping this?
- Do I have a place to keep it?
- Is this something I really want?
- Do I actually use it?

- Does it still look attractive?
- Is it still functional?
- Is it now obsolete?
- Is it damaged? Am I really going to fix it? How? When?
- Is it worth paying to store it?
- If I was looking for this and I couldn't find it, would it matter?
- Does it have significant sentimental value?
- How will I feel if it isn't in my world any longer?
- Who would care if I got rid of it? Does that really matter?
- What's the worst thing that could happen if I let it go?

Resist excuses for keeping things. When it comes to finding reasons to keep things, we've become pros. We tell ourselves, "But I might need this sometime in the future." That can be said for almost anything . . . and it's a good source of the problem you're experiencing right now.

Or we'll say, "It brings back fond memories." But is it worth cluttering up your valuable life today?

Or we'll insist, "I paid good money for it." Yes, but is it worth struggling to keep it just for that reason? Acknowledge it was a mistake or that its time of usefulness for you is over, and be free of it.

Other excuses you may need to resist are:

- "It's irreplaceable."
- "It was on sale."
- "It was my mother's."
- "It might be valuable in the future."

- "I plan to fix it."
- "Waste not, want not."
- "It was a gift from _____."
- "My child created it."
- "It's a project I want to finish someday."
- "They don't make things like this anymore."
- "I need to take care of it. Nobody else will."
- And the granddaddy of them all . . . "Just in case."

Challenge these thoughts. They are keeping you laden with too many excess items. These reasons may carry some value, but not enough for us to keep an overabundance in our limited space. Museums house items from the past. Libraries store books. Stores contain general household goods. We cannot have a museum, library, or store in our living spaces and still maintain a gracious, orderly, welcoming, and beautiful home.

Don't do it alone. Try to have a trusted friend in the room with you as you work. Professional organizers know that even when they are sitting passively in the room with a client, decisions flow more easily. They call it *body doubling* or *anchoring*. Psychologists find that the measures of stress levels (sweating, blood pressure, breathing rate) go down when another person is present. Just as misery loves company, so does decision making.

Try to avoid touching the items. Have someone else handle the items you are pondering, because physical contact with the item reestablishes a previous bond. Somehow, tactile connection reinforces the emotional connection with an item, even though our best judgment tells us to let go. As your helper holds up an item, say a quick yes, no, or maybe, and move on to the next item.

Flex your decision-making muscle. Making decisions is like developing a muscle. When you first start trying to make decisions, it's hard to do. It hurts. But after you get more and more practice, it gets easier and easier.

By the time you get around to handling the Maybe boxes, you will have developed more decision-making "muscles." Deciding about items will be much easier, your house will be much cleaner, and, in the future, you will be more decisive overall.

> We cannot have a museum, library, or store in our living spaces and still maintain a gracious, orderly, welcoming, and beautiful home.

Collapse any empty boxes. The cardboard boxes you assembled initially have the wonderful advantage of being able to be disassembled back to flat for easy storage or discarding. As soon as you empty a box and don't need it immediately again, flatten it. As you flatten boxes, your home begins to look better. It's easy enough to reopen the boxes if you need to. Flatten as you go!

KATHIE'S VIEW FROM THE MOUNTAINTOP

It was when she started collapsing the emptied boxes that Kathie began to feel the reality of what she had accomplished. The boxes were the last of her clutter.

When they were flattened and stacked against a wall in the garage, all the surfaces in her house were clear. More open spaces made it seem as though a fresh breeze had blown into her house. Finally, she felt that she had come to a spot

---

RULES OF STORAGE

1. Put like items in containers and label the containers.
2. Store items at or near the place where they'll be most often used.
3. Put the things most frequently used within easy reach.

Little-known fact: The amount of storage space is the most important physical factor in organization.

---

of completion. Now she had something worth maintaining. Now that the distraction of clutter was gone, she could see how to continue making improvements. Like an upward spiral, her enthusiasm for what she now knew she could do kept her going forward.

Where to Put the Stuff You Keep

Nobody is going to force you to get rid of anything. However, the laws of space will automatically limit how much you can keep. The laws of dignity and order will dictate how you store them. You are the final word about what you have room to keep and what you don't. Being in that position is your privilege; it's also a responsibility.

Rules of storage. Reality sets in when you actually start putting away things you have cleared from surfaces. Remembering that you have a finite amount of space, keep only things you need that will fit into your home neatly. Be sure to acknowledge the rules of storage:

(a) Put things in an appropriate container and be sure to label it.

(b) Store things at or near the place where they will be used.

(c) Put things used more frequently at a reachable height; store things used less frequently up high or down low; and put things that are rarely or never used in an outside or distant storage place.

Let's Talk Storage Turkey

Room for storage is the most important physical factor in organization. Pay careful attention to this fact. If you don't have enough room for what you've contained in the boxes, no organizational system is going to work.

The Pauli exclusion principle—a basic physics principle—states that two bodies cannot occupy the same space at the same time. Deep inside, we know this is true. It is impossible to keep an item if you don't have room for it. Yet we try to do it anyway.

1. Resist the temptation to squeeze items in somewhere.
2. Don't rent more storage space for overflow.
3. Don't leave an item just sitting around, until you can think of a place for it.
4. Step away from old nonproductive habits.
5. Form a good marriage between the amount of room you have and the number of items you want to keep.

Being the rather cerebral sort, disorganized people often find it hard to admit to themselves that important decisions about keeping "valuable" items can depend on something as mundane and practical as space. But it's true.

If you want to keep something yet you have absolutely no place for it, the only alternative is to either create an appropriate space for it or discard it. Usually, the way to do that is to get rid of less-important items. Avoid doing what Linda did as she tried to challenge, or at least bend, the Pauli exclusion principle.

Tale of a Talented But Misguided "Storer"

Linda was very efficient. So efficient, in fact, that she saved everything in a neat and orderly way. She used every available inch and was clever when it came to fitting in more. When she began to use a device that allowed her to compress plastic bags around items, she was able to save even more: clothes, stuffed animals, comforters, and many other fluffy items. She bought bed lifters so she could fit more under the beds. Her books were in double rows, thus doubling the amount her bookcase could hold.

Was her storing ability a good thing? Well, truth be told, Linda had a hard time remembering what she had and where she had it. As a result, she often bought replacements for her missing items—and thus had duplicates to store. Because her belongings were packed in very tightly, she had a hard time seeing and retrieving items she wanted to use.

As time went by, she lost track of how much she was accumulating. It wasn't until Linda moved and had to pack all of her saved items that she had an unexpected reality check. How had she saved so much? Long-forgotten items seemed to crawl out from the woodwork. Her remarkable ability to store items tightly had risen up to bite her. Now she either had to pack all of those things she didn't need, or take the time to make the decisions she didn't make long ago. And she sure didn't have time for that!

Don't do what Linda did. Make a decision not to keep everything, even if, by clever maneuvering, you can find a place to squeeze it into your house. Commit to living a serene and sensible, organized life, free of the stress found in an overstuffed house.

If you have an item you don't know what to do with, ask yourself a version of the question we suggested earlier: "If everything were perfect and my house were set up exactly the way I wanted it, where would this item live?" Depending on your answer, either discard it (because it does not fit into your perfect dream house), or go about creating the perfect place to store it.

When Beauty Becomes Its Own Worst Enemy

Sensitivity to beauty is often the cause of over-collecting. Here's what we mean by that:

Bennie saw beauty in everything. "Look at the design of this twig," she'd remark on a nature walk. Or, "Isn't it lovely the way the light reflects on this bag of marbles?"

KEY STORAGE SPACE QUESTIONS TO ASK YOURSELF:

How many drawers do I have?
How many cabinets do I have?
How many shelves do I have?
Are they enough?

She saw charm in things like an old teapot (only cracked a little) or a tattered feather boa. For her, an argument could be made to save almost anything.

Still, the combination of items that filled up her living area did not create a beautiful room. Every available surface was covered with these "beautiful" things. No clear surfaces remained. It looked junky.

What Bennie didn't consider was the appearance of the room as a whole. It was as if she was nearsighted and never lifted her eyes to see the unkempt jumble others saw when they entered her cluttered home.

As you work toward beauty, consider the room as a whole. Then consider the amount of space you are working with as you decide what to keep and what not to keep. If you are in a small house or apartment, you cannot keep as many items as you could if you occupied a large home with a garage. It's simple math.

Consider the way you want your entire home to look. Keep only the items that support your vision of an overall beautiful house. Discard individual items that do not contribute to the beauty of the whole. Or store them, if you must. But don't keep them on display. Those pretty things that clutter your house must find a home elsewhere.

The bottom line is this: It is hard to maintain a house that contains too much stuff, no matter how attractive or interesting each individual piece is. Remember that clear surfaces pull us toward order. Cluttered surfaces unbalance our organizational ability. Dedication to a welcoming and beautiful home helps us avoid the temptation to keep items that don't contribute to overall beauty.

She Fought the Garage . . . and Won

MJ tells this story of how she reclaimed her garage in only six hours, with the help of two high-school-age teens from a youth group trying to raise money to go to camp.

First, we drew a schematic of my garage, and I drew a plan of where I wanted everything to go (if my garage were perfect.) When I did that, I realized there were a lot of things in my garage that shouldn't be there—a broken lawnmower, chairs I had intended to reupholster, scuba equipment from a long-ago era, and holiday lawn decorations that were worn and cracked. The first thing we did was remove all of the things that I no longer wanted: the obvious trash, non-working machines, and outdated pool supplies. The next stage was a lot harder. We moved the big things to the out-of-the-way area predetermined and drawn on the schematic, then we took everything off the shelves. My helpers sorted tools, painting supplies, and gardening items. I went through the other stuff.

I bought matching bins that fit on the shelves and labeled each by family member. For family members not working with us, we labeled the bins with their names, adding the words "To Sort." We compacted each person's things into bins and neatly put them on shelves. We also tossed, donated, or recycled many things.

When everything had been removed, I swept and dusted the shelves. We didn't use any bins that were missing tops or were mismatched. All sports stuff went into a wooden toy box that sits open. Suitcases were nested inside each other.

I paid the students $10 an hour for six hours, so my total cost was $120 for labor, plus the money I spent for bins. And I spent eight hours of my time. But the garage is done and organized!

MJ and many others whose stories we have told have finally gotten their houses in order. The cheering fades and life goes on. But unless basic changes occur, slowly but surely clutter will drift back into the house. The homeowner will have lost not only the beauty of her home, but also hope that she can ever live a consistently clutter-free life. Now that the five-day plan is complete, section 2 of this book will unlock secrets your consistently organized friends apply so effortlessly and successfully.

Keep the Good Life Going

6

How to Live Happily
Organized-Ever-After

Keeping a harmonious home is like an athletic contest. You now know how to clear up the field on which the game is played; next is brushing up on the rules of how to play the game on a day-to-day basis.

First, ask yourself that all-important powerful question we have oft repeated: "If my house were perfect, how would I want it to look?"

To put it another way, if you went away for the day, when you came home would you want to see . . .

- uncluttered floor, seating surfaces, tabletops?
- no dishes in the sink or on the kitchen counter?
- the bed made?
- the bathroom(s) neat?
- laundry up-to-date—washed, dried, folded, put away?

- usable storage areas?
- something else special to you?

Suppose a friend unexpectedly dropped in; would you be comfortable inviting them in? We want your answer to always be a happy "Yes!"

Make It Even More Real

You may have heard of a vision board—a collage that displays pictures of a goal you are working toward. This would probably include pictures from magazines or on the Internet that in some way show what your dream home would look like.

You may work to create beautiful focal points in your house, then snap pictures and post them as a reminder of what you want to maintain. Sometimes, taking "before" pictures that later can be replaced with "after" shots works well as a motivator. Some people include written goals or motivational sayings or poems on their vision board.

These images can be glued to poster board, foam board, or even plain butcher paper, and displayed where they can be seen regularly. Of course, you will want to make it look attractive so it will inspire you each time you see it.

This kind of visual motivation works well for many of the creative but messy people who are working to transform their areas into neat and beautiful spaces.

Discovering the Secret of Maintenance

The following is a familiar but unfortunate story about life after initial organizing. Jeanette worked hard to get her messy house in order. And she succeeded. Proud of her accomplishment, she felt like she had really arrived. And she became somewhat rigid about every detail in the house.

But she thought that just because she had gotten the house neat, she had become an organizing expert. What she did not realize was that although she had developed a plan for her initial work, she had no plan for keeping it that way. She cleaned and neatened daily as she saw the need. That seemed to be the plan her successfully organized friends followed. For about four weeks, until the arrival of out-of-town houseguests, she was able to keep her order afloat. But the distractions of entertaining them somehow threw her off.

> **Maintenance is doing the same right things over and over again consistently, without undue thought or delay.**

After her friends left, her house began to slip slowly back into its previous unkempt state. Maybe it would have happened that way even if she had not had visitors. Jeanette was puzzled. What was going wrong?

In thinking about her problem, she found that maintaining a harmonious house requires deep-down changes in more than just surface areas. She found that she had to make some changes in how she thought and felt. Her time-use patterns had to change. And she had to address some of the habits of her family that were sabotaging her efforts.

Finally, she had to continue to tweak the storage issues of the house. Following the path we'll soon explain, she was able to bring her organizational ship around and move it toward the harbor of successful maintenance.

Solving the Maintenance Dilemma

The following are real-life stories from two women who realized that the initial cleanup is only the beginning of a deeper change. As you read the women's stories in their own words, take special notice of which strategies you think would work for you, as well.

Regina's Solutions

Regina had worked on her own style of basic organizing with one other person several times. "Afterwards it always felt so much better, though I missed some things or couldn't find them." (Note: The use of labeled boxes as in the Mount Rushmore method would have solved some of that problem.)

"The problem was that it never lasted long, but I have finally created some strategies that really work."

Be accountable. "As a disorganized person, I now ask someone to check, maybe monthly, on what's not working, and help me to see where I'm going off track. Then, if possible, that person can help me make a plan of attack for those areas." (Suggestion: Ask one of the team members you feel most comfortable with to come over occasionally for an evaluation.)

Incorporate new items quickly. "For me, the problem has often occurred when new items come in, and trying to incorporate them into the current plan. If that is not done pretty quickly, very soon my house looked like it did before the cleanup was started." (Suggestion: Be diligent in setting up labeled storage areas for groups of items, and watch out for buying items you don't need or for which you don't have a place.)

Avoid thoughtless stashing. "Out-of-control thinking leads to out-of-control stashing. Impulsively putting things just anywhere is great for the moment, but later I'd wonder where it was, and begin a frantic search. That resulted in more chaos, as I moved things about to find the item." (Suggestion: Always take a moment to ferry an item to its labeled storage spot.)

Create a good paper system. "I need the right kind of tools, mentally and physically. I am still searching for the right kind of file for me. Those deep, dark file folders in the deep, dark file cabinet just don't work for me. Things get lost in there." (Suggestion: Read the chapters on paper management in the book *Smart Office Organizing* by Sandra Felton and Marsha Sims.)

Regina recognized the importance of addressing maintenance issues. With her newfound systems and her commitment to them, she's well on her way to making organization a natural part of life that will keep her home neat and beautiful.

For Kelly, Every Day Is Like New Year's Day

Although the rules of organizing are the same for everyone, each of us applies them in a slightly different way. Kelly tells how she meets the challenge of keeping her house in order. It involves monitoring her mental outlook and setting up a workable schedule.

She writes, "When I started thinking about New Year's resolutions this year, I realized that for every day of my life as a recovering Messie, I need to renew my resolve. Each day when I wake up, I have to decide to continue on my path toward organization. Even if I faltered the day before, I have to pick myself up and keep moving forward." This is how that looks for her:

Use a fifteen-minute timer. "Some days, the dishes get piled up along the counter, as they used to, and I have to force myself not to get discouraged. I set a timer for fifteen minutes and focus on the dishes until they are finished."

Be realistic about time management. "For example, on days when I start to feel dread over the baskets of clothes that need to be folded, I remind myself that each basket takes only about ten minutes to fold and put away. That helps me get it done."

Seek group support. "I joined the online world of Messies Anonymous (found at messies.com) about a year ago, and my life has been steadily improving since then. The books and daily emails have really helped me along the way. Whenever I start to go back to my old habits, I have reminders to encourage me.

Keep on top daily. "The dishes and the laundry get done daily, even though I really struggle. Also, I try to put things back in their place as I go. Change is possible, but only if you daily make the decision to do it."

Schedule weekly activities. "There was a time when my house was so disgusting, I could not invite unexpected visitors in without a lot of stress. If someone called and said they were coming, I would have to do a mad dash through the house. Bedrooms did not get cleaned regularly (yuck!), and I didn't have any type of schedule for overall cleaning. Now, each week the house gets vacuumed, the kitchen floor gets mopped, and all three bathrooms get cleaned. Believe me, this is a big improvement."

Julie, another recovering Messie, writes that she has had a similar good experience with scheduling. "I implemented a schedule with four weeks of cleaning chores. Now I find that even with a demanding full-time job, I can get most of the housework done during the week and still have time for fun stuff on the weekend. The schedule and the organized home have made our lives significantly better."

They Did It—You Can, Too!

The testimonies of those above give us hope that if we concentrate on adjusting our daily lives in ways that meet our

---

TEN-MINUTE TIDY

Set the timer and see how much you can get done in ten minutes.

____ Empty the dishwasher.

____ Discard cans of food that are past the expiration date.

____ Vacuum a room. (Make it a quickie if it is a big one.)

____ Clean the sink.

____ Straighten a small part of a utility or linen closet.

____ Gather up all bills and set up a place to put them regularly.

____ Clear and beautify a table.

____ Dust the TV screen and other electronics.

____ Wipe the windows of your car.

____ Clear and vacuum the car.

____ Evaluate future plans for your garage and make one (or a few) changes.

____ Work on the car trunk.

Make your own ten-minute list. Post it on your wall or fridge and do one or two as the opportunity arises.

---

specific needs, tweaking as we go, we will develop a pattern of life that will eventually lead to a stress-free and orderly lifestyle, blessing us and those whose lives we touch.

The following four chapters spotlight keys to ensure that maintenance happens. The first of those, chapter 7, focuses on the key to it all—you!

7

Manage Yourself

Mary is a young mother with three freshly scrubbed children. Her house is always neat. Her children always have the right permission slips. She works full time, volunteers, and just seems to have it all together. How does she do it?

She would not be able to explain it to us. She's developed such automatic habits and schedules that she's not even aware of the fact that she's consistently following some very powerful maintenance rules. We, on the other hand, need to make ourselves constantly aware of these rules, and concentrate consistently on them until they become automatic to us, as well.

As You Change, the House Changes

You admit that you struggle to keep your house organized while others seem to be more successful. But why is it so?

Well, truly, just as there are differences in people's physical characteristics—height, weight, talents—there are differences in people's organizing views: the naturally tidy . . . and the naturally not-so-tidy (to put it nicely). Of course, most people are somewhere between those two ends of the continuum. In subtle ways that may not be obvious, the not-so-tidy among us tend toward disorder because we are more sentimental about things, we're more frugal, we're more creative about how to use "stuff." We usually have a more casual approach to life. These, and many other characteristics covered in previous chapters, keep us veering toward habits that add up to disorder.

Maybe order seems to come naturally to your neighbor, sister-in-law, friend, or colleague. They don't seem to struggle to keep their houses nice. For them, it doesn't seem to require much effort. And that's probably because

- They don't keep so much.
- They are Johnny-on-the-spot when they see clutter starting.
- They like to get projects completed as quickly as possible.

In a nutshell, they keep short accounts when it comes to handling organizational issues.

These personality traits hold the secret of maintenance. And if we will soak up some of those characteristics, just a few of the most powerful ones, and intertwine them deeply into our psyches, we will be able to maintain the hard-won order we've worked so hard to achieve.

Of course, everyone wants to be able to keep a nice house with as little effort as possible, and without making any changes in themselves. We value the way we are now. We like

- our casualness
- our intensity about belongings
- our love of things that others may find useless
- our ability to see possibilities in items
- our love of obscure beauty
- our focus on people rather than things
- our dedication to enjoying life in the moment without the distraction of jobs to be done
- our enjoyment of a variety of experiences, projects, and things

We tend to keep things for posterity that others would discard. We seem to treasure the past more deeply than others. We may even feel that when it comes to understanding life, we may be just a cut above some of our friends. Mark Twain even echoed this thought in his cynical statement "A neat desk is a sign of a sick mind." If we're truthful, we may admit to having a similar thought: "A neat house is a sign of a boring life." We hesitate to modify the unique characteristics that are so much a part of what makes us who we are.

However, the good news is that it really is possible to maintain order now that you've brought your house under control with the Mount Rushmore five-day team method. And you don't have to change your entire personality to make it happen. The key is to turn your attention to the habits you consciously or unconsciously have built into your organizing behavior. By making small but significant changes in just a few key areas of your life, you can reverse the cycle. Instead

> By making small but significant changes in just a few key areas of your life, you can reverse the cycle. Instead of watching your home drift into disorder, you can develop the habit of keeping an orderly and beautiful home, just like those tidy friends you admire.

of watching your home drift into disorder, you can develop the habit of keeping an orderly and beautiful home, just like those tidy friends you admire.

Because deep and consistent change involves abandoning ingrained and often-unconscious habits, you will do well to build in some extra outside supports. You might find great inspiration in reading additional books on organizing, participating in an online support group, working through a course from Clutter-Free University, attending organizing seminars, consulting with a professional organizer, or utilizing any opportunity that comes your way to give you a helpful kick in the pants when you need further motivation. Dipping into these can really help you stay on the right track as you work to develop new habits.

The Wonderful Law of the Vital Few

In the early 1900s, Vilfredo Pareto, an Italian economist, found that 80 percent of the land was owned by 20 percent of the population. Since that time, he and many others have found that this same 80/20 rule applies in many situations. For example, 20 percent of an employee's work will consume 80 percent of their time, and in our situation, 80 percent of the change in our houses comes from 20 percent of the change in our behavior. In other words, don't just work smart—work smart on the right things. Find those powerful "vital few" organizing habits, and it will cause a significant, long-term change in how your house looks.

Now *that's* an offer too good to overlook. Just remember that the few changes you make have got to be the right ones. In the next four chapters, in order to keep our efforts focused, we have spotlighted twelve powerful clutter-buster suggestions—three powerhouse rules per each of the four following chapters. These are the vital few. And in addition to those significant rules—we'll call them clutter-busters—we'll present some other important tips that you may want to adopt, as well.

So let's check out these clutter-buster habits. They, along with the additional hints and tips, may be just what you need to initiate little changes that make a big difference in how you live organizationally. And as you apply these practices repeatedly, they're sure to become powerful habits. Then watch the changes take root and blossom!

Clutter-Buster Habit #1—Stow as You Go

We've all heard the saying "If you get it out, put it back." That's a good start. But it doesn't go far enough. It should be extended to say, "If you get it out, put it back . . . where it belongs. Immediately!" A better way to remember it may be this: Stow as you go.

Say it. Sing it. Write poems about it. Do whatever it takes to embed this approach into your everyday behavior. If you apply only one rule to your life, make it this one. Do it, and you will find a huge improvement in the condition of your house. Probably more than 80 percent. Wow!

Clutter-Buster Habit #2—Catch Follow-Through Fever

As in golf, tennis, and other sports, lack of follow-through causes all sorts of problems. It's definitely true in the game of housekeeping. A lot of the clutter around the house is the result of a job that was left just 90 percent done. For example, shopping bags of groceries are brought home and, perhaps, taken to the kitchen, maybe even emptied, but their contents aren't shelved. Maybe clothing is taken to the bedroom but not hung or put in the drawer. Laundry is sorted, washed, dried, and folded, but never put away. The squeaking door is oiled effectively, but the can of oil is left beside the door. The broom leans against the wall under the hook on which it should hang. All of these are a-l-m-o-s-t finished, but not quite.

In this case, the well-known American proverb applies: "When a task is first begun, never leave it till it's done." And that means fully done. You won't have to go back after yourself and tidy up, because you won't have left things out in the first place. You will keep it up now rather than put it up later.

Clutter-Buster Habit #3—Practice the Thirty-Second Rule

Closely related to the previous rule is this one: If a task takes thirty seconds or less, do it immediately. For example, when you come home after shopping, don't drop your coat and the packages on the nearest chair or sofa. Instead, take thirty seconds or less to hang up your coat and move the packages close to where they belong. Or when you finish a bowl of cereal, place the bowl and spoon in the dishwasher. When you pick up the mail, walk to the trash can and discard the obvious junk.

Nothing Will Change Until You Do—More Proven Strategies to Move You Forward

Many thoughts and feelings relating to housekeeping have been woven into our lives by our experiences, even though we might not realize it. And they have a far bigger effect than most of us would guess.

But once you become aware of them, as you go about trying to maintain a really satisfying and consistent household experience, you can begin to challenge how they influence your behavior. The reason your tidy neighbor (friend, sister-in-law, etc.) can maintain an organized place on a regular

> **Keep it up now rather than put it up later.**

basis without seeming to sweat it is because she doesn't face a lot of these hidden issues in her life. As you recognize them and melt them slowly away, you'll find yourself empowered to succeed . . . without the struggle you've been experiencing. Consider whether the following factors play a role in your life.

Take Action . . . Making Plans Is Not the Same

Avoid being like Celeste, who always had big plans. She had a box of paper projects she was going to finish, a stack of paper that included a few bills to pay, a duster left out on the table because she intended to finish dusting later. Her house reflected a myriad of other small projects that were started and not completed. It was hard for her to clean up, let alone organize anything, because everything represented something she was in the middle of doing. She didn't want anybody to touch anything, and loudly and proudly proclaimed, "I have plans for that!" or "I'm going to do that this week!"

> "Talk is cheap. Deeds are precious."
>
> —H. Ross Perot

Celeste felt that she had to leave things out in order for them to jog her memory. "If I see it, I will remember to do it. If I put it away, it will disappear and I'll never remember!"

If you find that you are leaving things out so you can remember what you've started, don't be tempted by the dark side of remembering. Perhaps you are leaving it out as a testimony to your determination to do the job. But this approach clutters surfaces and does much to destroy the enjoyment of the house. Plan a time to do something, finish it, and put the item away. If you can't finish in the allotted time, put the item away and make a note to yourself to come back and finish it later. Take action. Then, stow as you go.

Overcome Learned Helplessness

Many messes are created from little undone things that are actually easy to do. We all understand why big jobs can be overwhelming. But what is the explanation for why we avoid—or seriously procrastinate—small tasks consistently?

Like a coil that has been stretched too far too often, our motivation has lost its spring. Failing at our prolonged overload of activities saps any can-do attitude we may have had. Because we feel helpless to do the little things, one plate left on the coffee table turns into a cluster of many, over time. We may walk by something on the floor many times, fail to reload the toilet paper roll, ignore a picture propped against the wall where it should hang, or fail to hang a jacket. The lack of a can-do attitude or a want-to-do attitude is the basis for much of what deteriorates into a condition that requires a team to undo the mess.

> "Do or do not. There is no try."
>
> —Yoda, *Star Wars*

By beginning to accomplish small tasks and moving on to larger ones, we'll see the power we possess to make important changes in our lives. We'll become slowly empowered again. Sometimes it takes a professional organizer or coach to regain that motivation to put forth the effort again. Sometimes it requires therapy. Sometimes just a friend who can encourage us to try, and praise us when we succeed, is all we need.

Care—Really, Really Care!

Somewhere in you right now, there's bubbling up a sincere desire to maintain a different way of life. That's why you picked up this book. You do care.

But do you care enough to sustain this new energy through the rough spots of making the long-term changes you so desperately want to make? You will have challenges, discouragements, mutinies, and who knows what else to contend with.

> "Oh, why not?!" Repeat these three little words to nudge yourself to do those little things you've been ignoring. When you see what needs to be done, say, "Oh, why not?" You'll be surprised at what will happen.

Only by truly valuing the wonderfulness of each cleared surface and by envisioning the life ahead, as the house comes fully around to order, will you be able to keep up the determination to do what's necessary to maintain it over the long run.

So value every battleground won. Keep those hard-earned territories clear of encroachment from "enemy" clutter. You will become disheartened from time to time. That is not unusual. Just pick yourself up, dust yourself off, and keep going. When you have created your new way of life for yourself and your family, you will love it. It will be worth it all.

Consider Depression

Professional organizers, though not psychologists, report that they see a lot of what appears to be depression in their work with clients who struggle with disorganization. The condition of the house is often enough to make any emotionally vibrant person fall into a depressed state. But frequently, it's apparent that the depression was what originally sapped the ability to keep the house under control.

Those with full-blown clinical depression are usually aware of it, and are hopefully already seeking professional help for the condition. However, those with low-grade chronic depression are often unaware that the lethargy they feel is the result of depression. They rationalize their lack of action or just call themselves lazy. Often, receiving help for that condition opens the door for improvement in the condition of the house and many other areas of life.

Be Aware of Distractibility

There are two kinds of distractions: external and internal. Distractions act like barnacles that drag down the progress of our housekeeping boat. Maybe a better metaphor is that being distracted puts obstacles on the maintenance track we are trying to follow, slowing and sometimes derailing our housekeeping train. Indeed, sometimes the house ends up looking like a train wreck.

The problem is that once the house has been basically organized, those who tend to wander in attention as they work find that they often leave a trail of disorder behind, even when they're trying to clean up. The piles they're clearing just end up in different places, rather than disappearing. Left-out cleaning products and equipment add to the clutter. They jump from one job to another, leaving many half done.

Sometimes the problem is that the house has not been set up to move things easily in and out of storage. Sometimes it's just that we're pressed for time. But in many cases, the real difficulty comes from an attention deficit on the part of the worker.

In recent years, professionals have realized that Attention Deficit Disorder (ADD)—with or without hyperactivity (ADHD)—is more common in adults than previously realized. It has been particularly overlooked in quiet but unfocused ("scatterbrained") women. When effectively treated, many women have found a newly acquired ability to accomplish goals without getting sidetracked.

Many men and women who experience difficulty in completing tasks successfully will never seek professional attention for the problem. Indeed, not all problems with attention are medically based. But in order to live the kinds of lives we desire, something needs to be done to address the difficulty. What to do?

For most people, just recognizing that they are using an ineffective hop-skip-and-jump method to keep the house in order is a step in the right direction. At that point, the best remedy is to take seriously the management methods suggested later in this book and other resources. Just because a person is distractible doesn't mean he or she is unintelligent and unable to manage positive changes in his or her life. Professor Nilli Lavie from University College London comments in an article about a test for distractibility, "Even if you are more easily distracted than others, you can decrease your susceptibility to being distracted."[1] Cementing a few powerful habits and systems into place can make a significant difference.

Learn the Tricks of the Trade

An adult who never learned how to "keep house" or file papers effectively is at a distinct disadvantage in the area of practical living. If the adult was raised in a messy house that nobody controlled, he or she has skipped learning in a crucial period of life. Or perhaps the house was beautifully maintained by paid housekeepers. Or maybe the "woman of the house" didn't want any participation of the children. Of course, some children resist learning, no matter how carefully taught.

How to keep house can be "caught" rather than taught, by observing how other successful housekeepers do it. Visit your friends and watch their approaches. Ask them questions. Even visiting houses gussied up for sale can be inspiring. Expose yourself to housekeeping success wherever you can.

Read books that explain the basics of good housekeeping, and start to apply what they teach. Don't think you have to apply all of the details they suggest. As suggested earlier, if you apply only a few of the key points—let's say, 20 percent of those ideas that you think can apply to you—you may find a wonderful 80 percent improvement in the condition of your house.

Overcome Overshopping

In the cases of about 15 percent of the people who struggle with the stuff in their houses, overshopping is a significant factor. Even when the problem is not severe enough to qualify at the "shopaholic" level, careless buying or buying of duplicates (because the original is misplaced somewhere in the house) becomes a significant problem. Too much stuff is the result of buying without consideration of its negative consequences.

Once an overshopper crosses over from the more logically based "looking" mode to the more emotional "buying" mode, sensible purchasing is difficult to control. Asking oneself questions similar to the ones asked earlier when making decisions about keeping items or discarding them helps to keep us in the logical arena. Some questions include:

- Do I really need this?
- Where will this go when I get it home?
- Will I be happy with this when I get home?
- Do I need to buy it in order to enjoy it, or can just looking at it now suffice?
- Do I really want this, or do I just like the experience of buying?
- Is this an unnecessary duplicate?
- Do I have room for this (without overcrowding)?
- Will buying this cause me trouble later? (e.g., No room for it, spouse angry about the purchase, budget busted.)

Carolyn wrote of progress she made in the following way:

On the way to Cleveland, we stopped at an outlet mall—a very dangerous place (for a shopper). I saw some really cute things. I was standing there, holding something up, trying to think about when I might use it. And caught myself. I said out loud that I was breaking one of my new rules about not getting anything, unless I had an immediate need or plan. I didn't buy anything. I was so proud of myself.

You may curtail overshopping by talking aloud to yourself or by utilizing a friend or coach to go along and verbalize these questions while you are shopping. Sometimes, just carrying a card with a pertinent question in your wallet or wrapped around the credit card is enough to break the shopping spell. Consider the impact of a card with the question, "Where will I store this?" or "Do I have a specific need for this?" One of those strategically placed reminders might just be what is necessary to bring shopping sanity to the scene.

Some recommend getting rid of (discarding, donating, etc.) one thing in the house for each new item brought in. Give this strategy a try, and see if it takes some of the pressure off of your overcrowded house.

A uniquely modern method is to take a picture of any item you are tempted to buy. Some find that simply having the item captured in this way and taking it home is enough to satisfy them.

Madeline, a compulsive book buyer, would impulsively buy books that she just "had to" have. "A trip to Barnes & Noble would cost me two hundred dollars in impulsive purchases," she says. To remedy this, she started taking pictures of the books she wanted to buy. "If I still want it in twenty-four hours, I have permission to go back and purchase it. And sometimes I do." But does she usually? "No." She laughs. "Normally I forget all about them. But I don't delete the picture . . . just in case!"

Instead of buying and having to stow all of the new books that she would probably never read, their pictures sit comfortably in her cell phone, where she can look at them at any time. "This works!" she says.

Plenty of good information is available through the Internet, books, counselors, self-help groups, etc., about how to overcome this all-too-common problem of overshopping. Your house will never be satisfactorily maintained as long as too much stuff is regularly brought in. Your house needs less, not more. Combining consistent disposal of excess and cutting back on what is brought in will make maintenance so much more successful.

Face the I-Hate-to-Get-Rid-of-Anything Feeling

Disorganized folks share a dread of having to part with "stuff." The method of de-cluttering that we use to face that fear minimizes having to make decisions about our beloved belongings. Eventually, as we clear surfaces and sort items, sanity begins to creep into our lives. We face the fact that thinning out the number of items in an overcrowded house is often a key element in regaining a comfortable normalcy.

Call it fear, discomfort, or nervousness. Whatever you call that feeling of dread, it can keep even the most capable, intelligent, or mature saver from wanting to open a box, drawer, or cabinet and deal with the contents. We care so much more than many people. It hurts us to think about parting with a beloved belonging. But it hurts even more over the long term to keep on living a life dominated by excess and clutter. So we must feel the fear and do it anyway.

> **We must feel the fear and do it anyway.**

Anabelle, a perky belle from the Deep South who was drowning in clutter, said, "I worked with a lot of charities that accept discarded items, and I know from experience that most of the money goes to pay their salaries." That was Anabelle's justification for holding on to everything. "I want to be sure that the person I give something to can use it and appreciate it."

Like Anabelle, sometimes we hold on to things because we are trying to control what happens to them after they leave our possession. If we focus too much on it, we become paralyzed. Anabelle unconsciously wanted to control who got the things she didn't want and determine whether their appreciation level was sufficient . . . and it was causing her to be paralyzed in her inability to let anything go. We say, Don't live like Anabelle! Let things go, and trust that they will get to the person who needs them the most.

As a professional organizer, Marsha employs this motto: I can control what's in my house and in my possession; I cannot control the world.

To help you embrace that healthy outlook, consider these tips, borrowed from "I've Got to Get Rid of This Stuff!" by Sandra Felton, available on Messies.com:

- Keep your overall clutter-free goal in mind—in vivid color, with strong emotion. Imagine it often!
- Have a pal with you as you make discarding decisions.
- Honor your long-time "friend" by making it part of a temporary monument. You may wish to put a note of thanks in front of the monument, composed of items to be discarded. Then leave this display in place for two or three days before boxing the items and removing them from your house. It sounds silly, but it can help ready you for the transition from treasure to trash.
- Take pictures of items you know you should discard. Keep them on the camera or computer, or in an album. Include some information about their history.
- Be bold. Send items you don't need or don't really want anymore to a new life, where they can be used, even if they're not going to the "perfect" person.
- Face tension by recording your stress level using an index of 1 to 10. Writing down a number to represent your stress level helps to make your task more rational and less emotional.

- If and when a flood of emotions sends you scurrying to retrieve your discarded possession(s) before they are gone, do this: Stop, relax your shoulders, and breathe ten times deeply, in through your nose and out through your mouth, counting each breath as you go. As the tension passes, revisit the thoughts that gave you the motivation to let those items go. Then move on to other activities.

- Tolerate the fear. It is very natural to have that emotion. If you are willing to sit with it pumping in your chest for a little while, it will eventually begin to subside, and you will find that you are becoming mature enough to handle it. It is perfectly all right to feel the fear of parting with belongings—as long as you follow through and part with them, despite the fear.

- Remind yourself about your final goal. Look at a picture of a house that represents what you want to achieve. Rehearse specifics of your plans. Read your visualization if you have written one.

- Be assured that as you do this more and more, your emotional distress will become less and less. As you see the house becoming clearer, you will appreciate the importance of what you are doing, and it will be easier to keep going.

Don't Be Too, Too Perfect

Perfection is almost impossible to spot in one's own thinking because it masquerades as one of our finest qualities. We consider ourselves to be a cut above many of our peers (even, or maybe *especially*, the neat ones). For example:

- Our superior compassion is seen in the house full of pets we have rescued.
- We recycle to an extreme, holding on to every recyclable scrap until we can dispose of it in the very most acceptable (but perhaps difficult) way.
- We air our beds daily to avoid mold growth, while less-health-conscious people are "foolish" enough to make the beds as soon as they arise.

In these and many other little ways, our perfectionist tendencies hinder our ability to move ahead easily in organizing. We are willing to sacrifice the condition of the house in order to live up to our "high" standards. Meanwhile, our houses and lives are troubled by too many pets to care for, piles of trash awaiting proper distribution, and unmade beds being aired. That kind of thinking has caused our aircraft of neatness and beauty to stall, crash, and burn.

Abandon those "admirable" but hindering ways of thinking. Toss them and move forward with a careless abandon and confidence that works for most of the neat people of the world!

Tighten and Guard Your Personal Boundaries

Being the expansive and openhearted people we Messies are, our tendency is to overdo in many areas of our lives, causing complications that we struggle with every day as we seek to maintain our homes.

We tend to go overboard in how we go about our hobbies, interests, recreation, and even jobs. If we quilt, we gather the amount of material that even a store would have a hard time handling. In sports, we obtain an overabundance of equipment that we'll never use in a lifetime. If we teach school, we collect reams of materials we might someday need. Home-schoolers fill their houses with wonderful projects. On and on it goes. It's all good stuff, mind you. It's just not good to try to keep it all in the home of a person who is seeking personal and family harmony for his or her life.

It is the same with time use. We dedicate ourselves more wholly than we should to an interest. We travel too far into whatever grabs our attention. Once we commit to a project, group, or interest, we dive in with enthusiasm. Whether it is Scouts, Sunday school, garden club, sports, or whatever, we take up the banner and lead the parade. But as a result, we don't have time to manage the basics of our lives, much less keep the house organized.

"One of the hardest changes I needed to make in myself was to limit myself to what was 'sensible' for our situation," said Jeanine. As exuberant people, we Messies much prefer walking on the unsuppressed "wild" side of life. That is part of what makes us uniquely interesting personalities. But we pay a price for indulging in over-the-top thinking and behavior.

Pull in your borders. Do less. Collect less. Store less. Buy less. You will find that your house will begin to pull around to "normalcy" in a natural way, and you will not have to struggle to maintain the beauty and order you have created in your hard-earned Mount Rushmore efforts. In the end, you will have more.

Enlighten Your Visual Alertness

As you know, our houses can drift into disorder without our even noticing it, until it is out of control. Things left out tend to fade out of conscious view the longer they are in the wrong place. We are surprised when we finally tune in and actually see the condition of the house.

To solve that problem, train yourself to really look at what is happening in the house several times a day. The primary way to do this is by hanging on tightly to those surfaces that you initially cleared of all debris, and perhaps beautified with a few appropriate items. Learn to love the peace and clarity of those cleared areas. The joy they bring you will urge you to maintain them. Anything plopped out of place will be an affront to the lifestyle you have grown to appreciate.

To further enhance your visual sharpness, try a few tricks to get you started in your visual alertness training.

- Focus on only one spot in the room. Close your eyes and imagine it in proper pristine condition. Open your eyes. Quickly clear away what is out of place.

- At night, open the curtains and blinds and turn on all the lights in the room. Now go outside and look in as if you are a visitor. You will "see" with an awareness you had not before and want to change it.

- Make a telescope of an empty paper-towel roll or your curled hand. Zero in on one spot and quickly attend to its needs.

- Take a digital snapshot. A picture somehow looks different from what we see with our eyes. Blow it up on a larger scale. Tackle that spot, then take an "after" shot to compliment yourself and to be a reminder of how the area should remain.

- Screw in light bulbs with higher wattage and turn on the lights. Bright light sharpens your visual attention.
- Invite someone over to the house. Subconsciously, you will begin to experience the condition of the house as you think your friend will see it.

The more you do these "tricks" to ratchet up your visual skills, the easier it will be to notice the condition of the house on a continuous basis. Being tuned in visually is one of the most powerful maintenance secrets of our naturally neat neighbors.

Above All, Seek a Higher Happiness

The condition of the house, whether good or bad, is the result of many small and often unconscious decisions. But what drives these choices? The answer is this: We always do what we think will make us happy.

Blaise Pascal, French mathematician and theologian, was right when he said, "All men seek happiness without exception. They all aim at this goal, however different the means they use to attain it. . . . They will never make the smallest move but with this as its goal. This is the motive of all the actions of all men."[2] Unless we are careful, this desire will fuel many small, unwise organizational decisions.

We procrastinate about putting things back where they belong because, at the moment, there's something else we would rather or should be doing. We walk away from the dishes on the dinner table. We keep boxes full of useless items. We ignore a half-finished project. We leave the bed unmade. And we do all of these because, for a nanosecond, those are the actions that deliver a flash of happiness.

DO YOURSELF A FAVOR

- Make sure you have enough light sources in your house (and garden). Take lighting seriously. Dim spots in the house are downers.

- Keep a magnifying glass in every area you store a reference book with minuscule print.

- Take self-care seriously. Tune in to your own body, your circumstances, your feelings, and thoughts. Be alert to what bothers you and take steps to remove any difficulty.

- Prepare for beauty. Have spots around the house for seasonal blooms, romantic bouquet gifts, and flowers you purchase for yourself. Have a variety of vases for different types of blossoms, but don't overdo on the number you possess (you alone know how many you have room to store). Remember to consider a favorable background to best outline or match your creation.

- Put your shoes on very early in the day. The pressure of shoes on the feet seems to signal to the whole body that you mean business for the day. And besides, having shoes on allows you to move ahead with jobs like taking out the trash.

- Jot on the spot. I would die without the white board on my refrigerator. It holds a running list of grocery needs and other items I would forget if I didn't make a quick note of it as the need arises.

- Take comfort seriously. Take what someone has dubbed "extreme care" of yourself. Get to bed on time, have adequate clothing for your lifestyle needs, get enough exercise, meet special needs—in short, remember that "If Mama ain't happy, ain't nobody happy." This is another way to say you need to keep yourself in good shape mentally and physically.

- Plan dinner ahead. Have all the food you need. Make sure you unfreeze what is frozen. Put something in the Crock-Pot. You'll be able to put a good meal on the table or have someone assigned and trained to take care of doing the deed.

There is a higher happiness that will bring, in the long-term, a life of harmony, beauty, and joy. You are renouncing the greater happiness for the lesser when you put off the tasks you really need to do. It's worth the pain of change in order to attain what you will later see brings true, lasting satisfaction. That kind of pleasure cannot be found in those fleeting messy actions—or inactions—that are stealing away what you really want. For your sake, for your family's sake, and for God's glory, we call you to embrace that greater happiness.

People who change the house one way or another and fail to change themselves will consistently be disappointed. That's because what will emerge is the same messy condition they worked so hard to escape. Re-cluttering takes us to a deeper disappointment than when we first began to clear up our house—because when we de-cluttered, we had hope that we could live a different life. It's disheartening to watch that hard-won order eroding.

But the good news is that as we enfold new habits into our lives, orderliness will begin to flow naturally into our environment. And like our neat friends, when we keep on top of things, it will look like we aren't struggling with clutter—because we won't be!

The next chapter offers housekeeping specifics to help you apply your newfound habits with success!

8

Manage Your House

After Rajda had a team clear her house surfaces, she noticed she was still struggling to keep the house organized. When she put her new habits into play in order to keep things put away, she found, to her dismay, that she didn't really have designated places to put many of her belongings. So slowly but surely, she emptied the boxes into storage areas of her house, applying a variation of the sort-and-store Mount Rushmore system her cleanup team had used. And slowly but surely, workable and convenient areas to neatly stow items began to emerge.

A house needs to be streamlined organizationally so it can be maintained with as little extra effort as possible. If you make the house function well by making sure that you have things grouped in places you can easily access, you will not be tempted to leave them sitting out as clutter. If your organizing system works well—i.e., you can easily locate what you need—you will save yourself a lot of energy and time looking for them. If it not only works for you but also looks good, your house will support, not hinder, your new lifestyle.

The following three super-important points—our "vital few" on this subject—will help turn the tide in the maintenance of your home.

House Clutter-Buster #1—Group Everything

Although this is one clutter-buster principle, it has three parts, each of which is essential. Wherever you go in your house, it is necessary to apply each one. You have seen them used before in the Mount Rushmore clean-up method. Now you can put them to use more broadly. They are the key to long-term and consistent maintenance of order in the house.

Rule #1: Group Things That Are Alike

Grouping things that are alike can be problematic for people who struggle with organizing, because it involves decision making. Being that we are perfectionists, what might be a pretty easy decision for some becomes something of a problem for us.

The problem hinges on the word *alike*. How alike do they have to be in order to go together? If you have a drawer for kitchen towels, does the oven mitt also go in there? How about the potholders? If you have a drawer for pens, should it include markers, as well? Should the group of prescription medications also include over-the-counter remedies and vitamin supplements? While some of these may be easy choices, they are the kinds of decisions that make the job a real chore for overly thoughtful, perfectionist people.

Since this kind of decision making has no concrete rules and varies from group to group, there is no right answer. Psychologists and professional organizers have found that those who are disorganized tend to make many small groupings of things that are very alike, such as separating pens, markers, and pencils. Those who are easily organized tend to generalize more and have fewer and larger groups, such as putting pens, markers, and pencils all into one container for "writing implements."

Any grouping is better than no grouping at all.

As you go around your house, which has become generally organized through the Mount Rushmore approach, you'll find other areas where you can make organizing easier by grouping items together into a center for those items. This will mean that you don't have to remember where each individual item has been stashed. Trying to remember where individual items have been stored in various places around the house is ineffective. Memory is not as reliable as the grouping approach.

"Where do we keep the alcohol, antiseptic ointment, Band-Aids, or adhesive tape?"

The answer is, "In the group of First Aid items." Of course!

"Where is the stapler?"

"Look at the office supplies." Naturally!

"Do we have an extra toothbrush?"

"Have you checked the box labeled 'Bathroom Stuff'?"

When you start grouping items, try to do so boldly. Velda's experience was this: "When my children were small, I grouped our bathroom supplies into plastic shoeboxes, each one labeled with a different body part. We had one labeled 'Eyes,' one for 'Ears,' one for 'Feet,' 'Skin,' 'Teeth,' 'Hair,' etc. All of the shoeboxes lived in the linen closet, and everyone knew where to put related items. It worked like a charm!"

Don't worry overly much about the details of how to make groups. Any grouping is better than no grouping at all. You can always make adjustments later as you see the need.

Rule #2: Place Groupings Into Correct Containers

Once you have your groupings gathered together and you've weeded out the duplicates, you're ready to put them into appropriate containers. Avoid using containers you already have that may not really be appropriate. Don't use grungy boxes, cracked plastic bins, or other unsuitable containers that you have lying around the house. You are committing to a new and upgraded way of life. Locate and buy, if necessary, containers—transparent, if possible—that are the right size for the amount to be stored. If you can, store items in matching boxes so you will feel proud when you look at them stacked neatly side by side. Many find that clear shoeboxes with tops are suitable for a lot of their groupings. They are often available at a dollar store.

Of course, you can use regular shoeboxes and, if you like, you can cover them with decorative paper for a cost-effective solution with extra pizzazz.

Cabinets for dishes and shelves for books are ready-made storage areas that are available in most houses. You may find that you need to call into service those magic white boxes for storing larger items. As you become tuned in to the concept of containerizing your belongings, the way to do it better will become clear. The main idea is JUST DO IT. Improvement will follow as needed. Consider Julie's experience:

I thought about how my house functions and what "centers" I needed. Past organizing efforts worked for a while, but then disintegrated because things didn't really have a specific home. Establishing centers was key. Before, I would sort of have things organized and I knew where everything was, but the rest of the family did not necessarily know where things were. Plus, centers made putting things back crystal clear. I didn't really know where each center would reside at first, but I clearly labeled the boxes of each. Then, when things were gathered together in the boxes, I could determine the space needed and the best location.

Rule #3: Label, Label, Label

The concept is simple: Write down on each container what is in each box. Make the lettering bold and clear enough to read easily. You may use labels designed for filing folders. Perhaps you will choose to use three-by-five stock cards. Some write on the box or container itself. The best choice is whatever works for you. Attach the label firmly to the container.

Do not succumb to the temptation to try to remember what is in each container without affixing a label. If you can't think of the right words to put on the label, write something that will suffice for the time being. Sometimes using the word "*Stuff*" helps move the labeling process along (hair stuff, nail stuff, electronic stuff, etc.). Occasionally, if you can't think of a word that summarizes the contents well, you may want to list a few of the items on the label. Again,

Done is better than perfect.

don't get stuck on perfectionism. JUST DO IT. Done is better than perfect. You can always go back and improve it later—or not. Sometimes enough is really enough.

Put the labeled containers in appropriate places. Using the grouping principle, put related boxes together. Create an office supply area, a work tools area, a cleaning supply area, a medical area, etc.

Items you use often should be located within arm's reach, in an area that's easily accessed. Store seldom-used items up high or down low. If they are never used but you have room and want to keep them anyway, archive them in an out-of-the-way place. If you run out of horizontal space, begin to use vertical space like the walls or doors by hanging things or adding shelving. If you have trouble recalling where some seldom-used items have been located, make a master list to guide you to those items.

> **The easier the system, the more likely it is to be successful.**

The more carefully you apply these three keys of organizing around the house, the easier you will maintain your home. The easier the system, the more likely it is to be successful.

House Clutter-Buster #2—Handle Paper

Jenna realized she had to take control of her papers. Papers, papers everywhere, and not any plan to control them . . . at least not one that worked for her. The condition of her house, in general, was turning around. But the one sticking point of clutter was the glut of paper that flowed into her life daily.

Fortunately, she had a model of paper order she could call upon. She approached her childhood pal CharlieAnn for some tips. And CharlieAnn, who knew about Jenna's organizing project, happily shared her secrets.

"It's not really complicated, Jenna. There are only two things you can do with a piece of paper that comes into your possession: keep it or get rid of it.

"Like most of us, you keep a lot of junk mail because you think you may want it later for a sale or something. You're afraid you'll discard something you'll need later, so you keep some things 'just in case.' When you do this, you end up putting useless stuff that should be thrown out or recycled into the same pile as important stuff, and it makes an even larger useless pile.

"You love the information papers," she continued with an understanding voice. "When we went on vacation together, you picked up brochures about attractions at every tourist stop because you imagined we might want to go to them. I'm not criticizing you. You just had a lot of dreams about what we could do. You live in a world of possibilities. You also save and make copies to give to other people. I tend to limit the amount of paper I get or keep so I have less paper to deal with.

"I suggest you go on a paper diet. When you get mail, stand over the trash or recycle basket, filtering out some and discarding it before you sit down. Keep only what you really want or need. That will do wonders for your paper problem."

CharlieAnn was right about the need to keep papers under control by sending what you can to a trash or recycle receptacle immediately. The paper you decide to keep should go into one of two different piles: "Action" or "Keep." *Action* are papers you need to act on. Papers in the *Keep* category are important papers that you will need for possible future reference (e.g., tax forms, birth certificates, health documents, etc.).

We have an easy plan to keep each of the two categories under control:

- ACTION—Keep *Action* papers in view where you can see them in some kind of to-do file. An open desktop file sorter keeps them easily accessible, but also keeps the area looking organized. Big-box department stores and office supply stores often have a variety of styles. Label each file folder with what needs to be done with that paper. You might have files labeled like this: "Call the water department," and "Send back signed to school," and "Order this."

- KEEP—Insurance papers, banking statements, tax info, medical records, school information, vital documents, and other papers you want to keep are candidates for the *Keep* pile you create as new papers enter your home. And they'll require quick transfer to a reference file or file cabinet used for many reference folders. It's important, though, to get the best filing cabinet you can afford. Be sure the drawers glide all the way out to their full capacity. Avoid file cabinets where the drawers only open partway. You'll be more likely to use the cabinet if it works well and has enough room.

  Each *Keep* paper needs to go into a folder, either one of its own or one for similar papers. File the folders by category. It works well to use the definition of a noun as your guide—person, place, thing, or idea.

Store files for people and pets in your home in a section of your filing cabinet labeled "People." In a "Places and Things" section of your filing cabinet, store files for things relating to the house, your rented storage unit, the garage you want to build, papers relating to your car, your appliances, etc. An "Ideas and Interests" section will hold files on hobbies, clubs, etc. You may want to use one color for the files or labels of each group.

The key to having a really useful reference file—one that you don't dread using—is (drum roll, please) to make a master list of files. On that list, you'll note each file you put into the file drawer. That way, you'll know what files have already been created, what you've named them, and where they're located.

For instance, when you add a *Keep* document that came home with your newly adopted puppy, you'll put it in a file labeled "Fido," and stash that file in the "People" grouping. On your master file list, you'll add the word *Fido* onto your list of files found in the "People" grouping.

A good way to make the master list is on a computer, so you can add and subtract files easily and neatly on the document. Keep your list in the first hanging file folder in the cabinet so you'll know where to find it for easy reference.

CharlieAnn added wise advice as she explained this system to Jenna: "Don't try to do it perfectly. Just do it. You will be much better off than you are now, struggling with all these piles. As you use the system, it will get even easier, and your papers will be under control in no time."

Jenna tried the system and found that CharlieAnn's prediction came true. The more she practiced, the better she got at managing her paper glut.

House Clutter-Buster #3—Love Beauty

Trying to keep an ugly house neat is drudgery. However, keeping a lovely house neat is a pleasure.

Beauty affects our behavior. In Japan, when two ATM machines—one aesthetically pleasing, and one not—were available side-by-side, the nice-looking one was rated as easier to use, even though the two were identical in function. Another researcher did the same study in Israel, where functionality is prized. To his surprise, the Israeli subjects rated the usability of the nice-looking machine even higher than the aesthetically oriented Japanese people.

In the book *Emotional Design: Why We Love (or Hate) Everyday Things*, Don Norman suggests a theory for why this is true. He believes that beautiful things change your emotions in a positive way, making you feel happy and less stressed. Your emotional state then affects your effectiveness in completing tasks. When you are happier and less stressed, most things you do are easier, and machines and other tools seem clearer and simpler.[1]

So an important conclusion of the research is that beautiful things are easier to use. Ugly things are less pleasing, annoy you more, raise your stress level, and generally make things harder for you. Reduce your stress and frustration levels, improve your ability to get things done, and heighten your feelings of happiness by surrounding yourself with more beauty.

When the tide of disorder begins to recede, it often exposes a shore devoid of charm or beauty. When the clutter is gone, you may find your decor needs a little sprucing up. Items may be a little battered, or the long-time frustration of the clutter struggle may have stifled the good taste that originally was displayed in your home.

One of the pleasures of making the change from cluttered to clear is the opportunity to discover your own personal taste, which you may have never fully developed. You'll want to discover the decor that will fit your own personality and tastes. As you move slowly forward, decorating the areas you clear, you will come to a tipping point where you will say, "This is great! This is what I have been working toward!" That is the time when your heart and front door will open to others to fulfill a longing for companionship that may have been buried for a long time.

Once you have experienced the satisfaction of that moment, you'll find maintenance much easier. Beauty, and the social interaction it encourages, inspires us to make whatever effort is required to keep order in place.

(Note: See chapters on how to discover your personal tastes in *Organizing for Life*, by Sandra Felton.)

Practical Matters

Practicality often plays a big role in keeping a house working well and looking good. Could some basic elements be adjusted in your home so that maintaining it will be easier?

Probably. Below, we've listed some commonly overlooked matters that may play a part in your life. You'll probably want to begin making some of the changes suggested that you feel may apply to your situation.

- **Make it easy.** If your house is set up in a way where it is hard to get things out and put them back, it will drift back into disarray. Most of the time, this shows up when too much stuff is stored in too small a spot, too much paper is stuffed in a file cabinet, or it's too much work to access what you need. That spells disaster when it comes to keeping order or filing.

  For a house to work easily, you need to leave as much space as possible around each item. You can see it. You can reach it. You can pull it down without starting an avalanche, and you can put it back easily. This can only be accomplished by paring down your belongings to what you really need on a day-to-day basis, not what you might need at some unknown time.

- **Maintain your inspiration point.** Erin stumbled on a secret of household excellence when she purchased a beautiful large candle surrounded by a flower ring for her coffee table. To enhance its effect in her otherwise cluttered room, she committed to keeping the coffee table polished and cleared of clutter. It gave her delight every time she glanced at it. Once she realized she had power to maintain beauty in that one spot, neatness began to ripple out to surrounding areas. Eventually, the whole house felt the influence of her creation of an initial spot of beauty on the coffee table.

Start with one inspiration point, feel your power, and begin adding spots that you are committed to keeping at the standard you have set for yourself, your family, and your home.

But how to get the family on board with your vision of a new way of life? The next chapter addresses that important part of maintenance.

9

Manage Your Family

Let's face it. Even if you have just one messy member of the family, that person can easily torpedo your best efforts to be neat. You may still be struggling to stay on the organizing wagon yourself, and you need their cooperation and support. Nobody can clean up the trail of clutter and confusion left by a whole group of slovenly people who don't buy in to the change you have made in your house. No one person has enough energy, time, or patience to maintain order under those circumstances. They are a little negligent here, a little slipshod there—it adds up quickly to a widespread mess, no matter how much you rush around behind them trying to right their wrongs.

Your family can be your biggest support. But if they're not, it's time to take steps to turn the tide by concentrating on the three big principles that will create a supportive and neat family.

Family Clutter-Buster #1—If Mama Ain't Happy, Ain't Nobody Happy

Home life does not run well as a democracy. Traditionally, women have carried the chief responsibility for the condition of the house. Along with that responsibility has come the privilege of being the major decision maker about the style and condition of the decor. Most often what visitors experience when they enter the house is primarily a reflection of her personality. If the "woman of the house" does not step purposefully into the role of household manager, the state of the house becomes unpleasant, drifting toward really messy.

"Housekeeping ain't no joke," as the maid, Hannah, says in Louisa May Alcott's *Little Women*.[1] To make it work well requires a lot of clear-eyed goal setting, persistence, and family management. Trying to manage others' behavior, especially while you're working to change your own, is difficult.

> Commit to the importance of long-term orderliness in your house and life. Seek out ways to accomplish it, with the help of your family.

Managing the organizational activities of the family doesn't come naturally to everyone, especially disorganized folks like us, who tend to be easygoing and friendly in our relationships. You need the willpower to begin to build into your personality and behavior whatever it takes to provide your family the organizational guidance they need, even if they resist it. They need someone who will run the house the way it needs to be run. For your sake *and* theirs. They need somebody who will take the trouble to train them in the right way.

Households that are satisfactorily maintained must have a strong captain at the helm. She keeps clearly in mind the destination for the house. She knows her crew, their personalities and skills. She knows she has to be wise, flexible, patient, humorous, creative, and loving. She cares enough to create a fair plan for the whole crew to follow. But if her ship of order consistently hits stormy waters or misses the port on a regular basis, Captain Mama ain't gonna be happy. She ain't scared to show it, neither, because there are times when she needs to be one tough cookie.

We are not suggesting a Captain Bligh approach, pushing the unhappy crew to mutiny. Sure, they may grumble and object about having to get off the gravy train of careless living they have enjoyed riding. Who wouldn't? Every successful mom expects that and does not let it deter.

But if you look around at your successfully organized friend's family, you will probably see that it is very, very possible for a family to work together harmoniously for their mutual benefit in keeping the house organized. You may see some unsuccessful approaches to avoid, as well.

Commit to the importance of long-term orderliness in your house and life. Seek out ways to accomplish it, with the help of your family. Then Mama will be happy, and, rightly done, so will Papa and the rest of the family.

Family Clutter-Buster #2—Let Each Person's Disorganized Behavior Boomerang Back on Him or Her

It is unlikely that everybody in the family will immediately buy in to your new realization that organized living is far superior to disorganized living. The kids are not as mature as you are and have gotten used to careless habits at this point. As in many areas, they need training.

If your spouse is basically disorganized and has grown used to living that way in an uncontrolled house, he will likely resist changing what has become a comfortable, if frustrating, lifestyle for him.

The whole family has suffered in some way from the messy situation in the house. When the house doesn't look good and doesn't function well, frustrations and inefficiencies abound for everybody.

Of course, you will communicate verbally your desire for them to get on the neatness bandwagon. You may talk to them casually about it; have a sit-down, face-to-face meeting individually; call a family meeting; or all of the above. You may set up chore charts. Hopefully those will work, although often their value is short-lived—just enough to get the activities started. Usually more than talk is needed. One powerful way to make sure they know that it is in their best interest to become neater is to fix it so that their own messiness becomes more and more problematic for them.

Here's how it works: Whatever messes they make should make their own lives—not yours—more difficult, whether naturally or with a little bit of enhancement on your part. Don't rescue them from their carelessness.

If you have talked more than you feel is necessary with less-than-stellar results, it is time for a paradigm shift in your approach.

For instance, don't help them look for items they consistently carelessly misplace. As part of your new approach, tell your charges that if they do not stow things when and where they should be, you will be happy to take charge of their belongings. State to the kids what you plan to do if such an occasion should occur (as it undoubtedly will). Then do what you told them you would do. Let them know that they will have to ask for misplaced book bags and homework next time. Let them know ahead of time that if it continues after that, they'll find these things in mystery or inconvenient locations. For example, if wet towels are left on the bathroom floor and you have communicated the problem—but to no avail—move the offending items to the middle of their bed (in a plastic bag if you're squeamish about damp sheets). Try gently kicking dirty socks left on the floor under the dresser. When they run out of socks, they will notice. Be cheerful. Say nothing about what is happening. Your behavior will speak loudly for you. You have now moved away from talking and have begun a much more powerful method of communication. If you are pleasant and consistent, you will be surprised at the result.

June had a system. When her children were younger and it was time for them to clean up, she would get a pillowcase and prepare to "kidnap" their toys and such, and then start counting. "You have five seconds to come and get your stuff" she would say before she started counting down. "Five . . . four . . . three . . ." By the time she got to three, children would come flying in from every direction, grabbing their stuff.

June's put-everything-in-the-pillowcase system worked because the children didn't want their good stuff in a bag with their sibling's "junk." "I used this system because it worked," she laughed. Her children, now with children of their own, still remember the unique way their mom got them to clean up.

Other possibilities are these:

- Put homework papers left on the dining room table in an out-of-the-way place, like the laundry room or a random closet. Say nothing unless they ask you. They will begin to get the picture.
- Book bags dropped by the front door can be tossed into the garage. Say nothing.
- Make up any unmade beds, but include a few books and/ or papers (or some other items of choice) under the covers. Of course, be pleasant and say nothing.

The point you are making is that if they don't like the way you handle their messes, it is in their best interest to put things where they should go rather than deal with where they might end up otherwise. Often they will get the message and not say anything. But if they complain that they have been bothered and inconvenienced by how things are working out for them, don't fuss or become defensive. (Ha! Like you aren't bothered and inconvenienced daily by their messes!) The ball is in their court. Suggest that they may handle their belongings in a way that works better for them. They may very likely become agitated. Nobody likes to change. The secret is for you to remain reasonable, friendly, calm, and above all, confident. You will be tempted to give up. Don't. Adjust this approach according to age and personalities, but don't back down. This method will initially require effort and imagination on your part, but in the long run your family will learn to be neater and more organized, so it will benefit everybody.

For more strategies on this, see *How to Organize Your Life and Family* by Sandra Felton.

Family Clutter-Buster #3—Become a Management Genius

You saw how well a team effort worked for getting the house cleared of clutter. Now you can rally your family to be your team and maintain the house on an ongoing basis. It takes time. It takes effort. But it is more than worth the investment you make in learning to manage your family in this area.

Our best chance of influence is when we apply the following at the right time:

- Patience
- Imagination
- Creativity
- Determination
- Consistency
- Persistence
- Humor
- Love

Post signs, such as *Stow as you go.*

Repeat sayings like "Let's catch Finish-Up Fever" or "Many hands make light work."

Play games: "Let's see how much we can put in place before the piggy timer goes off."

Recite silly poems: "Boys who are neat lift the seat."

Use strategic sequencing, a first-this, then-that approach:

- "As soon as your room is picked up, you can have a snack."
- "Clear the table quickly, then come into the living room for games."
- "After you put your laundry away, we will go shopping."

Display picture reminders: Take a picture of the way an area should look and post it close by. Or draw a little reminder, such as a hand dropping clothes into the hamper.

You might even want to have each child sign a contract for chores he or she promises to complete. The added benefit is that when they become adults, they will respect a signed contract.

More Helpful Info Follows

In addition to the three key family principles, we need to note other practical matters we may have been overlooking. Note which of the following factors seem to play a part in your life, and begin making changes you feel may apply to your situation.

Delegate Not Just for Your Sake But for Theirs

You want and need help around the house. You not only want the family to quit being a part of the problem by making messes, you want them to actively be a part of the solution by participating in the maintenance efforts of neatness and cleanliness. You owe it to them to teach housekeeping skills they will use the rest of their lives. In addition, they need to learn the concept of accepting their part of the responsibility for their surroundings, both as members of your family and later as adults. Yes, dreams can come true. Here's how to train them.

First, you have to overcome your own reluctance and doubt that it will work. Stop yourself when you find yourself thinking

- I don't have time to show them how to do it.
- I can do it better myself.
- They cause me too much hassle.
- They don't have time to help me.
- I enjoy doing this.
- I'm not a good example.
- I tried it in the past and it didn't work.
- It's too much work to keep them on the job with me.

But it's crucial to get them on board with keeping the house in order. In fact, it's the best way for all of you to have a home you enjoy, a place you'd all like to share with friends.

Delegating takes planning. Don't hand out assignments haphazardly. Keeping in mind that children's abilities vary, start training when they're as young as possible. If your children are already older, start where you are. Developing a work mentality is imperative.

Children at two or three love to "help" Mommy and can be trained to put away their toys, dust with a sock on their hand, help with laundry, and feed the pet. Older preschoolers can help with food preparation, putting away groceries, and setting the table. From six to eight they can be called on to fold and put away laundry, take out trash, and vacuum and mop. At ages nine through twelve, they can do laundry, help with washing the car, do the dishes, and fix simple meals. A well-trained teen should be capable of handling almost any chore at home. If Mom is absent from the home for a while, she should find things pretty much as she left them on her return if a fourteen or older teen has been in charge. Keep in mind that teens often have very busy schedules that need to be considered when scheduling their household activities.

Communicate to the family about the changes you will be making. Don't be discouraged by resistance. Keep your cool and confidence.

Set up an appropriate plan, where jobs are distributed fairly, taking into account the ages and schedules of each family member. Don't try to be perfect in this decision making. You can always adjust as you see the need. Write down your plan.

When you delegate, don't abdicate. Train where necessary. And stay involved in overseeing. Check up from time to time. Acknowledge your family members' successes and reward them in some appropriate way. That can be as simple as, "Your room looks great. Do you want to invite your friend over to see it?"

Don't Mess Up Your Relationship While Cleaning Up Your House

Children require one approach. An adult, quite another— even though you may think he or she behaves like a child when it comes to making messes.

Let's note some important facts to begin with. More and more, men have stepped up to the plate when it comes to household chores. Research shows that in today's world, men contribute about the same amount of time to family chores as the working wife. Let's give huzzahs and kudos to those men who fit those statistics. Their wives are fortunate, indeed.

But not all men belong to that group. Sometimes women who tend to be messy themselves attract those who enjoy the same casual approach to organizing.

Just because you have decided to change your habits and maintain order does not mean everybody else in the house will get the same desire at the same time. They might not even like the change. You may find you will have to discover ways to deal with various messy situations that arise with your family.

Let's say it's your roommate who constantly leaves his or her stuff where he or she finishes with it—things such as a glass on the living room table, underwear on the bathroom floor, spilled sugar on the counter, etc. Obviously, you are sick and tired of the time and effort used to pick up after another adult. What's more, you feel that it's unfair and disrespectful to you.

You are getting tired of complaining about the situation, and he or she is undoubtedly getting tired of hearing it. Prepare to talk seriously about the situation. Communication is the key. Let your roommate know that it is important to you that the common areas of your home be kept neat. What he or she does in her private space is not your concern.

When the husband is the Messie, explain that, for a woman, helping to keep the house nice is a very significant way to show love for her. Some guys have little or no concept of how important it is to a woman for him to help keep the house nice. In a sense, the house is her larger self. Without his realizing it, ignoring this aspect of life together reflects a lack of either respect or understanding. Explain how important it is to you, and ask him to invest (a manly kind of word most men appreciate) in the relationship by taking your need seriously in this area. Explain that you don't want to feel like a mother nagging a kid. You are looking for a partnership.

Name two or three of the most significant behaviors he can begin (perhaps some of the habit actions, such as "Stow as you go") to make you happy, and let it go at that. Keep it simple and straightforward. No need for him to "take the vow" and promise that he will do better. In many cases, just the fact that you have voiced your feelings in this way will probably encourage an improvement.

But maybe talking will not be enough.

Regardless of the type of relationship you have, in the event that problems continue, as they often do, a second approach may be useful. Switch from talk to action.

Wherever possible, don't rescue your partner from the negative consequences of his own sloppiness. Don't complain about the negligence or explain your actions. If your partner steadfastly fails to put his keys on the hook you have provided by the door, don't help him look for them. Don't participate in the frantic rush to find a misplaced work paper or wallet. This may seem unkind. But in the long run, it will prove to be best for you both and for the relationship.

Complications will arise. You may hear:

- Excuses: "I left my toothbrush down to air it out."
- Accusations: "You leave things out, too, you know!"
- Demands: "Leave my things where I put them. I want my jacket on the floor."
- Attacks: "You are obsessed with this neatness thing. Chill out!"
- Criticism: "You have become such a nitpicker."

Go slowly. Be patient and understanding. Respond calmly or, preferably, not at all. Understand that change of any kind is very hard to tolerate. It will take time for you to learn this technique. Though you may doubt it from time to time, it will be worth all this effort.

Life is too short to live in a frustrating environment, and too short to treat your most important human relationships carelessly. It takes wisdom to balance the two. As Kipling said in his poem "If," "If you can keep your head when all about you are losing theirs and blaming it on you . . . you'll be a man, my son."[2] Well, maybe not the "man" part, but you get the idea.

The final area of management we need to control is how we utilize our time. The next chapter addresses time and how we can best use it in our organizing quest.

10

Manage Your Time

Time-management is a somewhat misleading term, since time flows steadily and inexorably forward without any ability on our part to control its forward movement. What we *can* control is how we function in that flow.

We can choose what activities we focus on and how we delegate the use of our energy. So time-management is really a specialized kind of self-management. Nothing more. Nothing less.

Those people who are strong at determining and maintaining focus on a few important activities get a lot accomplished. Those who can't quite decide what's most important tend to become easily distracted. They find that although they work hard and arrive tired at the end of the day, little of significance has been done.

The goals we set work best when they are

- Specific. Don't just plan to "clean house." Name particular tasks you want to do.
- On a deadline. Determine when you aim to have a specific task done.
- Written. This makes goals more specific and shows seriousness.
- Tracked. Create a way to check off each goal as it's accomplished.

Once we have narrowed down what we want to do, we are ready to engage the body in actually accomplishing something. The following clutter-busting strategies will help us overcome the inertia that is so much a part of disorganized living—whether because we are overwhelmed, overworked, or just generally disheartened—and will help us use our time wisely.

Time Clutter-Buster #1—Nibble Away at Encroaching Clutter

Simple little habits can have powerful results. Begin weaving a few small but consistent changes into your behavior and watch the house change.

Adopt the Thirty-Second Rule

The thirty-second rule is designed to put a stop to the messes you make as you move through the house. When you come in with packages in your arms, do you dump them by the door? Do you drop clothes on the floor? Or fail to hang up the towel after a shower? Leave a plate by the sofa?

Walk away from an unmade bed? Neglect putting the toilet paper roll on the holder? All because you don't want to take the time to take care of the situation the right way at the moment?

Just a few of these little neglected maintenance activities add up to one messy house. But these messes will never appear in the first place if you simply adopt this idea: If it takes thirty seconds or less to accomplish an activity, do it right away.

To get a feel for how much time thirty seconds is, watch a secondhand on a clock or sing a song that takes thirty seconds (such as "Happy Birthday," sung twice in an energetic manner, or once very slowly). You will be amazed at how breaking the habit of leaving a trail of objects behind you will keep your house from nosediving into clutter. And the change will happen almost effortlessly!

Applying the thirty-second rule is closely akin to a previous suggestion, catching the Finish-Up Fever. A person with Finish-Up Fever has a strong urge not to leave part of an activity hanging. No sir-ee! They are hot to cross all their T's and dot all their I's on all parts of a job before they move on. It's not a bad idea to use this idea to encourage kids to catch Finish-Up Fever.

Fan the Fifteen-Minute Habit

Sometimes we need to start small. Nola discovered power in the habit of setting her kitchen timer for only fifteen minutes. She set that amount of time each day to finish up her organizing projects or to straighten up her house that had been previously organized with the help of her team. It made a remarkable difference.

Though fifteen minutes a day was not quite enough time to get into some serious organizing or deep cleaning, it opened the door to the creation of a lifelong habit of setting aside time just for organizing into her day. When her house was neat and organized, and she used the thirty-second habit consistently, fifteen minutes was about all she needed to keep it maintained. If she needed more time, it was not hard to continue on with getting things back in order. Or if she had a project that required more time, like emptying boxes or organizing cabinets or closets, the fact that she allotted a doable fifteen-minute time frame helped to just get her started. Although she gave herself permission to stop after fifteen minutes, she often kept going until the task was done.

For Valerie, using fifteen-minute time limits helped her overcome a job she'd felt paralyzed to complete. Her house was overcrowded with furniture inherited from her recently departed father, and she just could not face dealing with it. So she'd been doing nothing to correct the problem. Eventually, though, she found herself able to commit to fifteen minutes a day. And although she was emotionally exhausted after fifteen minutes, just starting helped break the ice of decision making. She began to make consistent steps toward neatness and order.

Raylene found a powerful weapon in her organizing arsenal—fifteen-minute family participation. Once she introduced what she called the Daily Fifteen-Minute Flurry to her family and enthusiastically led the charge, the accumulating clutter in the house started to clear.

Consistently working for fifteen minutes a day is much more powerful than it appears, because of what it leads a

Set your timer for whatever you can commit to:

- THE 15-MINUTE FLURRY
- THE 10-MINUTE TIDY
- THE 5-MINUTE FRENZY

Little things mean a lot in time management. Commit to the 30-second rule or the 15-minute habit. Throw in "Stow as you go" on a regular basis, and your organizing projects and daily maintenance will become easier—instantly!

person to discover. Many who try the fifteen-minute habit have a story about what just starting it taught them. For the first time, they face hidden emotional and mental hindrances that had been avoided by inactivity. They realize that they fear change or have serious procrastination problems. They face the stronghold that sentimentality has on them. As they ease into organizing fifteen minutes at a time, they feel the power they had relinquished for various reasons somewhere along the way returning, replaced by a growing can-do attitude.

It All Adds Up

Doing the math is an eye-opener to those who have been avoiding handling maintenance consistently. Only fifteen minutes a day for six days a week adds up to an hour and a half for the week, and about six hours for the month. Plus, once started, the organizing often extends beyond the fifteen minutes. Some people find that they want to do fifteen minutes in both the morning (maybe before work) and evening (after work). If you engage family or friends, as well, your fifteen minutes is expanded exponentially. Wow!

Time Clutter-Buster #2—Routines Are the Sleds That Move Progress Forward

Being free spirits and creative types, disorganized people avoid routines. But they don't like being disorganized. Experience shows us that you can't have it both ways. Commit to introducing a few simple routines into your day and you will be more free to indulge your creative side.

Morgan's Laundry Problem

Laundry for her five children was the bane of Morgan's existence. It was a hateful chore that had to be done often. She'd tried every approach she knew. She tried doing it first thing in the morning. That didn't last. She did it last thing at night. To no avail. She used every approach possible, but the job never got done well, and she hated it.

Finally, she decided to analyze the steps of her laundry activities and see how she could streamline it. That led her to change her approach entirely. Instead of going through the detailed steps of gathering the laundry from around the house—sorting, washing, drying, folding, and putting away— she set up a new routine. She gave each child two baskets with their name on it. When one was full, the child was responsible for taking it to the laundry room to be washed. No more sorting per person, since each kept his or her things separate.

She washed, dried, and returned the clean clothes to the child to be folded and put away. Meanwhile, the second basket collected more dirty clothes. They kept rotating them in that way. Training the children to follow this procedure was not only helpful to her, but it was good training for the kids.

This new approach freed Morgan from carrying the burden of unnecessary activities. By analyzing a particular problematic situation, you may be able to devise a whole new, more workable system. Ask friends what works for them.

To devise a system that will work for you, consider these steps:

1. Define the nature of the problem. What part doesn't work? What bugs you?
2. Brainstorm what could make it better—maybe a change in scheduling, a different piece of equipment, etc.
3. Buy necessary equipment and put it in place.
4. Educate those involved about the new way of doing things.
5. Make and post charts, signs, and other reminders.
6. Be alert to make it work as planned, and tweak parts when necessary.

Carla's Mail Dilemma

Maybe the word *routine* raises your ire. You don't want to be rigid. You value your spontaneity. So let's take another approach. Instead of gritting your teeth and establishing a lot of new routines, just begin to fold new habits into your life. Little by little, that will do the trick.

Consider Carla's story. Because she was tired when she came in from work and hated to make decisions about how to handle problems she might find in her mail, she avoided looking at her letters by putting them into a pile. Bills became overdue. She missed good sales. Once she even misplaced a jury summons and was unable to respond. Birthday cards got tangled in the pile until her birthday was long over. IRS and social security letters awaited attention there. She never knew if time bombs lurked in that pile.

Carla finally created the simple habit of walking her mail to the trash can, discarding the useless stuff immediately, and opening what was left. Then she divided the rest into two labeled boxes on her desk labeled "Action" and "File" to be handled later. She put a sticky note stating a few words about the action to be taken. Anything she could not decide about went into the *Action* box to be looked at again. Setting up that simple system and following that one habit made handling the mail a much easier job. One by one she added other simple new habits, and it made life much less stressful and more productive.

Time Clutter-Buster #3—Use Time-Management Tools That Fit Your Need

If we look at Pareto's law of the vital few, we see that it applies equally well to how we manage our time. Of the things you do during your day, 20 percent are really the big guns of effectiveness. That 20 percent produces 80 percent of your results.

Identify and focus on those things. When the fire drills of the day begin to sap your time, remind yourself of the 20 percent you need to focus on. If something in the schedule has to slip, if something isn't going to get done, make sure it's not part of that significant 20 percent.

Posting and Highlighting Important Information

A blockbuster idea is to magnify the three (or so) most important things that you want to accomplish in the day. They are the most critical of your top 20 percent. Write them in large letters on a piece of paper with a little check-off box next to each one. Post them in a prominent place. Check them off as they are done.

Lists

Probably the most important time-management tool is a simple to-do list. Your list could take the shape of

- A vertical list, written on a piece of paper with the date at the top.
- Quadrants, each with its own topic, such as Go/Call/Do/Buy or Important and Urgent; Important, Not Urgent; Urgent, Not Important; Not Important, Not Urgent. This method makes your list more powerful. Be flexible. Name the quadrants as they fit your need.

Go/Call/Do/Buy Quadrants

Go	Call
1.	1.
2.	2.
3.	3.
4.	4.
5.	5.
6.	6.
Do	**Buy**
1.	1.
2.	2.
3.	3.
4.	4.
5.	5.
6.	6.

- A Things-To-Do file. Fill a desktop hanging file folder with file folders for each activity you have to do that's tied to paper. The folder tabs become your list, and you won't lose the papers that need to be acted upon.

Planner

No successful daily/weekly/monthly/yearly planning happens without a planner of some sort. Planners come in many formats to accommodate our lifestyles and preferences. They may have one page per day, two pages per week, two pages for the entire month, or some other design. They vary widely in size. Choose one that works for you.

If you need to keep a lot of information, you may want to use the page-per-day type of planner. If you need a lot of time to be visible at once, you may need a planner that shows several months' activity in a large space.

Many people now use a computer program (such as Outlook), a Smartphone, a tablet, or some other electronic device to keep calendar items organized.

Additional Tips to Weave Into Your Life

Unlike household clutter, time clutter is invisible. Because of that, it requires concentration about how it really works. In addition to the three main clutter-busters of time management, be alert to the following factors.

Tailor Your Multitasking Wisely. Psychological experimenters have found that subjects often can't handle doing two things at once well. In experiments, subjects perform poorly when multitasking because of the time and attention required to transfer from one task to another.

But most of us who live in our modern hurly-burly world participate in multitasking with happy abandon. Indeed, we feel we must. Busy mothers consistently cook while signing school forms, advise on homework questions while answering the phone. We all listen to the radio while driving, or we watch television while folding clothes. Many office jobs require the same level of multitasking. Activities such as stapling pages between answering simple questions are what constitute low-attention-level tasks. When we participate in two or more of these at the same time, usually no harm is done.

Productivity begins to fall dramatically, however, when we try juggling higher-level activities that require concentration, such as writing a report while fielding phone calls. In order to make the best use of your time, where possible, plan to accomplish jobs that require concentration during uninterrupted time.

The bottom line about multitasking is this:

- You can mix activities that require a low level of concentration.
- Be careful when trying to mix a low-level activity with a higher one.
- Consciously avoid trying to do two higher-level activities at a time. Finish one before starting another.

Be Alert to Vampires. Vampire bats live entirely on blood from animals. They stealthily nip a spot and sip while the animal sleeps. Though each bat takes only a little, many

TOP TEN TIPS FOR DE-CLUTTERING
AND STAYING DE-CLUTTERED

10. PAUSE TO PLAN before you begin any organizing activity. Write, talk, visualize, or in some way decide specifics on how you are going to proceed.

9. FAN THE FLAMES OF DESIRE. Solidify your goals with inspirational pictures, group support (online or face-to-face), books, etc. Keep your enthusiasm high.

8. START EACH DAY STRONG. Make the bed, get fully dressed first thing, have a complete breakfast.

7. CHANGE YOUR PERSPECTIVE. Focus on clearing surfaces instead of removing clutter.

6. JETTISON EXCESS. Don't keep more than you can easily manage.

5. GROUP AND LABEL at every opportunity. Make it a habit to store like things together.

4. USE A TO-DO LIST religiously. Group by topics and prioritize.

3. SAY "OH, WHY NOT?" when tempted to procrastinate. You'll be surprised at what you can get done.

2. DO A LITTLE EVERY DAY. Use a timer.

1. STOW AS YOU GO. Immediately return things to their proper place after use.

sneaky bats slurping from the same animal can add up to a lot of blood loss. Meanwhile, the animal is unaware that anything is happening.

Time use has its own vampires that steal valuable minutes. And those can add up to hours without our being fully aware of how much time we are losing. Usually they are entertainment related, such as television, social networking, computer games, reading, listening to music, surfing the Internet, and other things that feed our reluctance to get up and do something probably less interesting but definitely more constructive.

A time vampire may even be a valuable activity that is easier, and therefore more appealing, than tending to the house. Sometimes other people's demands distract you. Beware when you see any of these creeping up on you.

Dream your dreams. Set your goals. And don't let time vampires weaken your ability to accomplish them.

Set Progress in Motion

Some short, low-level activities are valuable because they precipitate other productive activities. Loading a dishwasher. Putting a load of clothes into a washing machine. Turning on a Roomba cleaning robot. Do them, and you can start the bowling ball of accomplishment rolling down the alley. You set it up, then walk away and it does its thing. Your time is well spent when you set these up to do what they were designed to do.

Sometimes progress is set in motion when you make a phone call to have someone come to the house to do a job that for some reason you cannot or will not do, or just have not done. A quick telephone call to hire a professional can pay off in hours of work being done. That's a big payoff in time-management.

Anchor-Drifting Goals

It is interesting to examine perspectives of organized people. Janet confesses, "I can't rest if I haven't completed everything

I planned to do. Sometimes I will be lying in bed and something I needed to do will pop into my head. It's hard to go to sleep then."

Janet—Miss Organization, it seems—was happy to talk about one of her favorite topics: keeping order in her life. Janet explained that she keeps a running tally in her head of what she wants or needs to get done each day and mentally checks them off as she goes. She keeps on top of what needs to be done, and thereby avoids many of the complications of procrastination.

A big part of Janet's approach is that she relies on her memory. Experience teaches us that we who struggle with disorganization take risks when we try that. What we can do is substitute for memory a simple list system that works for us, enabling us to enjoy the sane, productive life we are seeking.

Janet's mental list of goals for the day is well thought out and heavily embossed in her brain. For us, uh . . . not so much. But the solution to our problem is beautiful in its simplicity.

An old Chinese proverb says this: "The faintest ink is more powerful than the strongest memory." Jump on the bandwagon of that concept and ride it to a more organized life. It's simple. Be sure to utilize a planner and a to-do list, with three priorities for the day.

Written goals and steps will give you the effective focus Janet carries around in her head. Otherwise, jobs that you would do, could do, and should do just drift around in your consciousness, coming into focus on a spotty basis. The result is spotty accomplishment.

You want to get your life under better control. This simple method will anchor those jobs you neglect, not because you procrastinate, but simply because you don't remember them at the time you could do them. Give it a try. Get a three-ring binder, and label it "My To-Do's." Make it attractive, then write your list of six things to accomplish.

Go Change the World

You want to change the world. There is no doubt about it. Everybody wants to do something significant, to have made an impact with the life they have been given. If cluttered living has dulled the glow of a dream you once had (or almost had), now is the time to move the debris, dust the vision, and return to a version of that all-important question: "If everything were perfect in my life, what wonderful thing would I do?"

> The legacy we leave is not just in our possessions, but in the quality of our lives. The greatest waste in all of our earth, which cannot be recycled or reclaimed, is our waste of the time that God has given us each day.
>
> —Billy Graham

Perhaps you would exercise your artistic ability, start a business, volunteer at a local hospital, or go back to school. Or perhaps you would like to bless the lives of others by spending time with your friends, creating a beautiful garden, or leading a study at your church. Create memories for a lifetime for your children. Make an impact.

Time is the canvas on which your life is painted. Each day is a brushstroke of the legacy you are creating. Clear the clutter of things and unproductive actions. Streamline the path to your best life.

No matter how young or old, the opportunity is yours to begin what may have seemed impossible. Don't hesitate any longer. You have the tools. Call in outside troops. Follow the game plan to order. Leave a legacy, not a mess.

A Final Word

You have some very powerful tools in your hands—tools you can use to finally clear the clutter that has been dragging you down for a long time, and that can empower you to maintain the wonderful harmony and order you are seeking. Furthermore, if you have the time and desire, you have what it takes to apply these ideas to helping others in need.

Again, let's return to that all-important question we began with: "If things were perfect in your organizational world, what would they be like?"

Stop a moment and retrieve the vision you have been building as you read the how-to's of this book. Set your goal in writing. Call in outside help to get the house under control using the Mount Rushmore method. After the five-day plan is complete, continue working to empty boxes into organized storage. Finally, begin the behavioral changes and habits in yourself and others that will maintain the welcoming, comfortable, beautiful home of your dreams.

Appendix

Helpful Resources

MESSIES ANONYMOUS (www.messies.com) is a group designed for support of those who struggle with clutter. Founded by Sandra Felton in 1982, the Messies.com website offers support with:

- The Organizer Lady daily reminders
- Internet groups covering various interests related to organizing (ADD, twelve-step, moms, hoarding, and more)
- Information about getting started with organizing
- Audio classes on various topics with experts
- Resources, including information about all of Sandra Felton's books
- Links to local organizing groups following a twelve-step program to conquer disorganization

- The Super-Flipper—a kit for developing a schedule of maintenance—is available through Messies Anonymous.

CLUTTER-FREE UNIVERSITY (www.clutterfreeuniversity .com) offers live, interactive, online classes at www.clutter freeuniversity.com and provides help to overcome disorganization through:

- Structure
- Accountability
- Personalized help and attention
- Daily homework and feedback
- Classes available: Organizing 9-1-1, Power Over Paper, Clutter-Free Forever

Books

- *Conquering Chronic Disorganization* by Judith Kolberg
- *Organizing Your Day* by Sandra Felton and Marsha Sims
- *Smart Office Organizing* by Sandra Felton and Marsha Sims
- *Get Organized and Clutter-Free!* by Skye Askew
- *Organizing Plain and Simple* by Donna Smallin

Blogs

- Get Organized Wizard.com—www.getorganizedwizard .com/blog/
- Simplify 101—http://creativeorganizing.typepad.com/

- OnlineOrganizing.com—www.onlineorganizing.com /BlogList.asp?sort=organizer&schedule=58

Other Organization-Related Websites

- http://organizedhome.com/
- http://unclutterer.com/

Other

- To help people with hoarding issues—a topic beyond the scope of this book—refer to *What Every Professional Organizer Needs to Know About Hoarding* by Judith Kolberg. It's good for nonprofessionals, as well.

Notes

Introduction

1. Frank I. Luntz, *WIN* (New York: Hyperion e-books, 2011), chapter 1.

Chapter 4: Putting the Plan Into Action

1. Susan Jeffers, *Feel the Fear and Do It Anyway* (New York: Fawcett Columbine, 1988), 227.

2. William Wordsworth, "Daffodils," 1804.

3. John Muir, *The Yosemite* (Berkeley, CA: University of California Press, 1988), 192.

4. Ralph Waldo Emerson, Journal, 1936.

Chapter 7: Manage Yourself

1. "Are You Easily Distracted? A New Psychological Test Measures Distractibility," May 30, 2007, www.sciencedaily.com/releases /2007/05/070530085016.htm.

2. Blaise Pascal, *Pascal's Pensées,* trans. W. F. Trotter (New York: E. P. Dutton, 1958), #425.

Chapter 8: Manage Your House

1. Don Norman, *Emotional Design: Why We Love (or Hate) Everyday Things* (New York: Basic Books, 2004).

Chapter 9: Manage Your Family

1. Louis May Alcott, *Little Women* (Rockville, MD: Serenity, 2009), 96.

2. Rudyard Kipling, *Rewards and Fairies* (Garden City, NY: Doubleday Page and Co., 1910).

Acknowledgments

Special thanks to Michelle Ogletree for her really good feedback; to Nanette Holt who labored like a yeoman with us in the editorial trenches to make the book super clear and thoroughly practical; and finally, to Lonnie Hull DuPont for keeping us on the straight and narrow in an editorial way.

Sandra Felton, The Organizer Lady, is a pioneer in the field of organizing. She is the founder of Messies Anonymous, a self-help group dedicated to helping chronically disorganized people who struggle with clutter to find order, dignity, and even beauty in their lives. She is the author of a variety of books on the subject of organizing one's house and life, and applies proven principles to the subject of organizing homes and small offices using the upbeat approach that has become her hallmark. Visit Sandra at www.messies.com.

Marsha Sims is the founder of Sort-It-Out, Inc., a professional organizing firm in Miami, Florida. She diagnoses problems and prescribes solutions with a practical wisdom developed in the field and brings seventeen years of hands-on experience to the subject of office organizing. Opening one's office door is an intimate matter. Marsha enters that door with a profound respect and high regard for those who have trusted her enough to invite her into their lives, whether in personal or business spaces. Visit Marsha at www.sortitout.net.